ABORIGINAL
WORDS
OF AUSTRALIA

ABORIGINAL
WORDS
OF AUSTRALIA

Reed New Holland

Published in Australia by
Reed New Holland
an imprint of New Holland Publishers (Australia) Pty Ltd
Sydney • Auckland • London • Cape Town

14 Aquatic Drive Frenchs Forest NSW 2086 Australia

218 Lake Road Northcote Auckland New Zealand

86 Edgeware Road London W2 2EA United Kingdom

80 McKenzie Street Cape Town 8001 South Africa

First published in 1965 by Reed Books Pty Ltd
Reprinted in 1974, 1975, 1976, 1979, 1981, 1983, 1987, 1988, 1990, 1998
Reprinted by Reed New Holland in 1998 and 2001

Designer: Luisa Laino
Cover illustration: Kim Roberts
Typesetter: Midland Typesetters
Printer: McPherson's Printing Group

National Library of Australia Cataloguing-in-Publication Data:

Aboriginal words, of Australia

ISBN 1 87633 416 9

(1) Aborigines, Australian–Languages–Dictionaries.
1. Reed, Alexander Wyclif, 1908–1979.

499.15

20 19 18 17 16 15 14

CONTENTS

INTRODUCTION

Readers of this book will no doubt realise that only a small proportion of the words used by the aborigines of Australia can be included in a book of this size. There were hundreds of languages in use among the tribes. The most that can be said for such a compilation is that it gives a fairly representative selection of aboriginal words from all parts of the continent, arranged both in English and aboriginal alphabetical order, with a short selection of phrases and sentences, and an indication of the origin of the words. The curious, and those who are in search for names of houses, children, boats, and for other purposes, will find a rich treasury of words native to their own land.

There were two main divisions in the languages of the aborigines, northern and southern. The northern region comprised the Northern Territory, the north-western region, part of central Australia, and the Cape York Peninsula. In this large area there was little affinity between the various languages.

The main division of the southern tribes also consisted of many different languages, quite dissimilar from the northern tongues, but having some affinity in structure, and with a number of words which were used by separate tribes whose vocabulary was in other respects quite distinct.

Unfortunately there has never been any uniformity in recording the spelling of aboriginal words. The *Australian Encyclopaedia* quoted an early example of seventeen vocabularies of the Wiradhuri lanaguage collected by one research student in which the word for 'water' was rendered as kaling, kul'en, karlee, kalleen, galling, kalling, kalli, kullung, kaleen, kalun, karlin, karlee and gulli, and by others as guleen, gulleen, culleen, cully, callein, colleen, collin, cullie and calle. Obviously it would be impracticable to show all the variants of the words in the present volume. On the other hand, well-known variants are quoted after the spelling accepted (often arbitrarily), and also indexed in alphabetical sequence and referred back to the main entry.

Some linguists substitute 'k' for 'c' in spelling aboriginal words but this has not been followed here, because the change in many well-known words (korroboree for corroboree, koolabah for coolabah) would be confusing to the general reader. The spellings given, whether using 'k' or 'c', are those in common usage.

In earlier comprehensive lists there has seldom been any indication of the area of use of the words quoted. In the present work some attempt has been made to show the location of the words. The superior figures shown in the Aboriginal-English section refer to the following areas:

1. Western Australia
2. South Australia
3. Northern Territory
4. Victoria
5. New South Wales
6. Queensland
7. Tasmania
8. Central Australia

The use of a superior figure does not however preclude the use of the word in another area. On the other hand it may have been used only in a single small district, and therefore unknown in the wider territory. The omission of a figure implies either that the exact source of the word has not been located, or that it was in fairly widespread use.

The Aboriginal–English is more comprehensive than the English–Aboriginal section. The words relating to natural phenomena, parts of the body, simple pronouns, numerals up to four (after this number a word meaning 'many' was usually employed), and other important subjects, have been recorded by many students, and little would have been gained by providing a large number of variants in the English–Aboriginal section.

Listing of animals, birds, fish and crustaceans, insects, plants, reptiles, shellfish, snakes, trees, and weapons and tools, are given under these general heads in the English–Aboriginal section. For convenience, these listings follow the alphabetical sequence of the aboriginal words and their meanings, rather than the reverse. At the same time the English and Aboriginal words, and their meanings, appear alphabetically and individually in the appropriate sections of the book.

Many books and periodicals have been consulted in the preparation of the lists. The most valuable were those that were published early in the history of European exploration and settlement, when missionaries, amateur anthropologists and philologists, and others rescued some of the vocabularies before the tribes became extinct. It is impossible to acknowledge all the sources, for an odd word or two has sometimes been taken from a single book. Grateful acknowledgment is made to the following publications:

Edward E. Morris: *Austral English* (Macmillan and Co. Ltd); K. Langloh Parker: *Australian Legendary Tales* (Angus and Robertson Ltd); W. Ramsay Smith: *Myths and Legends of the Australian Aboriginals* (George G. Harrap & Co. Ltd); K. C. McKeown: *The Land of Byamee* (Angus and Robertson Ltd); Ursula McConnel: *Myths of the Munkan* (Melbourne University Press); and the following works long out of print: A. M. Duncan Kemp: *Where Strange Paths Go Down*; E. I. Watkin: *Australian Native Words and their Meanings*; G. Taplin: *Folklore, Manners and Customs*; W. H. Willshire: *The Aborigines of Central Australia* and *The Aborigines of South Australia*, and early issues of *The Science of Man*.

Mention must also be made of the Australian Institute of Aboriginal Studies (Box 553, Canberra) which as one of many activities, concerns itself with the study of Aboriginal linguistics, including the standardisation of spelling and pronunciation.

With its many shortcomings, some of which no doubt are attributable to the compiler, and others due to a study which can never become an exact science, the publishers hope that the little book will be useful as well as interesting. To those who wish to pursue the subject further we commend the advice of Sidney J. Baker in his excellent work *The Australian Language* (Angus and Robertson) pp. 218–9: 'The most extensive work. . .is probably *The Australian Aboriginal Dictionary* by W. Bishop (1929) which is in MS. form in the Mitchell Library, Sydney. This contains many thousands of terms, but is rather a catalogue than a dictionary. No effort is made to indicate the dialects or districts to which the words belong. An incomplete although interesting *vocabulary of Aboriginal Words and Names* was published in 1916 by James J. Baylis, but contains some patent inaccuracies. Another work—again incomplete and misleading—in MS. form is a *vocabulary of New South Wales Aboriginal Dialects*, compiled by members of the staff of the Mitchell Library, Sydney (1908).'

To these, and the books mentioned above, we would add the collection by Sydney J. Endacott entitled *Australian Aboriginal Words and Place Names*, now published by Georgian House, which is currently in print in an enlarged edition.

A.W.R.

WORD LIST
ENGLISH–ABORIGINAL

A

abduct: pettin
aborigine: arrilla; daen
above: booloot; kerau kiath
abundance: (abundant): kembla, ngruwar
abuse (verb): ngaiyuwun
acacia: boobyalla; coobah; mulga; sallee
accompany: wallin
ache (verb): wirin
adolescent girl: wirreebeeun
adultery: moruldun
affection: woorinyin
afraid: blukkun; gerringong; gnoyalanna; jirrand; wai-i
after: ung
afternoon: kulkawura
again: kangulandai; munganye
against: nerambo
agreement: monomeeth
ah!: yakkai
alarm: blukkun
alas!: eeo eeo
albatross: pookanah
alive: tumbe
all: ngruwar; parehana
almost: ngak
alone: konkinyeri; naityi
along: illpun
also: inye
altogether: ipminger
always: kaldowamp

amateur: myall
ambush: gerringong
ancestor, totemic: pulwaiya
ancient: ranwul
anger: ngraye
angry: cooler; ngrakkuwallin

ANIMALS:

alait: dog
alli: dog
aloota: kangaroo rat
alpugi: kangaroo
arinya: kangaroo
arrurrer: kangaroo
arutchie: native ferret
baan: dog
baarlijan: platypus
bailaquar: bullock
bamburr: kangaroo
banjora: koala
banya: black-tailed possum
beereek: native cat
berontha: flying squirrel
biggoon: water rat
bilba: bandicoot; bandicoot rat
billeang: bat
bindar: kangaroo
bohra: kangaroo
bokkar: dog
bonelya: bat
boolgana: kangaroo
boondar: kangaroo
boorbee: native bear
buggoo: flying squirrel

bukkandi: native cat
bullula: kangaroo
bunderra: black wallaby
burra burra: sheep
burrendong: native bear
butterga: flying squirrel
carbora: native bear
coolabun: native bear
cowirrie: rat
durda: dog
erawar: rock wallaby
ertargwar: rat
gaya-dari: platypus
goomai: water rat
goonur: kangaroo rat
inger-godill: horse
innar-linger: echidna
jirrah: kangaroo
joatgba: kangaroo
kaddely: dog
kangaroo: kangaroo
kekuyan: spiny ant-eater
keli: dog
kinie-ger: native cat
koala: native bear
koob-bor: koala
kooim: kangaroo
koola: kangaroo
koonappoo: mouse
koongarra: kangaroo
kooraltha: spotted ferret
kroman: kangaroo
kulai: echidna
kulan: possum
kulla: koala
kundal: dog
kur-bo-roo: koala
kur-rook-ar-rook: koala with young
kwimpy: kangaroo
kyema: kangaroo
leena: possum

longootpar: kangaroo
lottheggi: bat
madba: kangaroo
madhi: dog
maikurri: bandicoot rat
mammerool: dog
mangaroo: phalanger
mari: wallaby
marloo: kangaroo
miga: dog
minyun: kangaroo
mongan: a mammal
moochambilla: kangaroo
moodai: possum
mooroo: bitch
motthari: seal
munthu: kangaroo
murra-wunda: climbing rat
murri: kangaroo
myorli: small red kangaroo
naggi: dog
narahdarn: bat
nargoon: koala
ng'rui moch: native cat
nilee: bush rat
nurrumpi: koala
omalwin: kangaroo
pademelon: scrub wallaby
pargi: wallaby
piggi-billa: echidna
pongo: flying squirrel
porlta: possum
potoroo: kangaroo rat
pulyara: long-snouted rat
pundeol: mouse
pundi: dog
punkunduli: bandicoot rat
puppa: dog
purnung: dingo
purtia: kangaroo rat
qualpar: large rat
rekaldi: water rat

taranna: wallaby
tarmaroo: possum
theen-who-ween: platypus
thirlta: kangaroo
tjukaro: kangaroo
tuan: flying squirrel
umorra: rat
uwurta: bush wallaby
wallaby: small kangaroo
wallaroo: large kangaroo
warreen: wombat
warregal: dog
warrew: wallaby
warrie: dog
warrigal: dog
waroo: kangaroo
warta: wallaby
wenjoitj: kangaroo
werunnunn: dog
windawityeri: bullock
wirlpa: hare
wirngill: native bear
wombat: a marsupial
wongguri: ring-tailed possum
wuka: flying fox
wurgulin: short-legged kangaroo
wutta: dog
wyehoota: possum
yallara: long-eared bandicoot
yangatan: native cat
yangor: kangaroo
yarraman: horse
yarraringy: possum
yarri: native bear
yarunmundule: bat
yelka: dog
yukunder: kangaroo

ankle: tunge
anoint: tyetin
another: kangulun; kaso; kultha; kutsha; yammine

answer (verb): werentun
ant: prilde; teeta; wirpa; yerra
ant, bulldog: carltooka; kotbityerowe; nalgarmyeri; tokiejonburnba
ant, small black: minga
ant, sugar: yeramba
ant, white: mirta; odunepa
ant-eater: kekuyan; piggie-billa
anxious: pairpin mewe
any: hii hii
apart: konkinyeri
appear: pappora; terpulun
apple, kangaroo: gunyang
arm: erricha
arm, lower: puthawing
arm, upper: tyele
armpit: elunba; ngiakkai
arrange: yuppun
arrive: puntin; tainbarilin
arrowroot: wiinki
as: luk
ascend: loru; wangkin
ash, Moreton Bay: ilumba
ash, mountain: warreeah
ashamed: kulyulaikin; palthawangalnappa
ashes: narcoola; quinja
ask: kurrin; reytyunggun; wankin
asleep: oongarra
assemble: torarin; yuntuwarrin
at: noondha
athletic: carrangall
attack one man: throttun
aunt: barno; konkea
aunt, maternal: num-ba-di
Aurora Australis: Pillie thillcha
autumn: marangani
awake: kinma
away: konk
axe, stone: mogo
axe, wooden battle: woggara

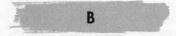

B

baby: birra-li, milla milla; puka; umbacoora; wangoora

baby girl: quei-marla-goobita

back: artippa; moorapoo

backbone: ngiampi; polgumpi

bad: ngontha; thulga; wadleena

bag: dilly; wanka; yergutta

bag, food: koorngoo

bag, kangaroo skin: kumbi; punauwe

bag, skin water-: attower

bag, string: goolay; mera; wullanti

bag, water-: gulli-mayah

bait: berley

bald: dooliba

ball: pulyugge

ball game: pulyugge

bamboo: omil-dadgee

banana bird: nutam

band, forehead: garbai

bandicoot: bilba, punkunduleol

bandicoot, long-eared: yallara

bandicoot rat: bilba; punkunduli; maikurri

bandicoot, spotted: mikurri

bank: engorra; thacka

banksia: werite

banter: borak

bare: merate

bark (verb): ronggummun; kunakunakasno

bark, tree: bingarra; opera-yenpa; pulthar; yulthi

bark hut or **shelter:** dardur; gunyah; humpy; wurley; mia-mia

barking lizard: wulla-barl

bark of kurrajong tree: mooroomin

bark vessel for holding water: wirree

barracoota: kyena

barramundi fish: anka

barter: munmunde

barter shell: arama; wela

basket: beenak; tareema

bat: billeang; bonelya; lottheggi; narahdarn; yarunmundule

bathe: boge; pullun; yakake

battle axe; wooden: woggara

bay: thalme

beach: booner; minna

beach, sandy: koynaratingana

bean tree: enunta; irtalie

bear native: see koala

bear, native, with young: kur-rook-ar-rook

beard: ngernka; yaran

beardless: tolai

beat (verb): began, marnin, mempin

beat time: winamin

beautiful: dandloo; endota; nunkeri; wambalano

beauty: eleebana; elleenanaleah; lowanna

because: marnditye

bed: tudhuki; yoyangi

bee: warra-nunna

bee, brown: ollo

bee, honey: kuyan

bee, small black: cooba

beech tree, white: binburra

beefwood tree: illginga; mubbo

bees' nest: calimpa

bees, sign of: coorigil

beetle, black: ouratta

beetle, orange and blue: noora-gogo

beetle, water: boongurr

before (in front of): ngunggurank

before (of time): ungunai
beg: raraityungun; wankin
behind: karlowan; mangka;
    nananook
believe: wurruwallin
bellbird: jumjum
belly: atnitta; bingy; kurunto;
    mankuri
below: moru
belt, man's: wakoola; waywa; bor
    (the 'belt of manhood', invested
    during initiation ceremonies)
beneath: maremuntunt
bend (verb): kertun; leewun
bend (trans. verb): menaikundun
bend, river: ngarte; thuckara
bent: pipa
beside: thinana
between: tarangk
bewitch: millin; ngadhungi
beyond: moondah
bidyan ruffe (fish): kooberry
big: booral; buntor; ecmurra;
    grantali; murna; proi
billy: wolbitta
bird: otayba

BIRDS:

   aroo: cygnet
   arunta: white cockatoo
   atyimba: emu
   baiamul: black swan
   barook: teal
   bartill: parrot
   beela: black cockatoo
   beereegan: quail
   beerwon: swift
   benalla: musk duck
   berallah: musk duck
   berigdra: orange-speckled hawk
   berontha: crow

berrimilla: kingfisher
betcherrygah: budgerigar
biaga: hawk
bibbi: tree-runner
bilbungra: pelican
billai: crimson-wing parrot
bilyana: wedge-tailed eagle
bilyarra: eagle
bingami: mopoke
boobook: mopoke
boogoo-doo-ga-da: rain bird
boolongena: emu
boolungal: pelican
boondoon: kingfisher
booran: pelican
bootoolga: blue-grey crane
brolga: native companion
bullai bullai: green parrot
bulln-bulln: lyre bird
buln buln: green parrot
bulooral: night owl
burrandool: quail
burrengeen: peewit
carnka: crow
chipala: whistling duck
chippia: duck
cockalella: white cockatoo
currawong: bell or black
    magpie, donkey bird, or crow
    shrike
curriequinquin: butcher bird
curringa: black duck
deereeree: willy wagtail
degeen-boya: soldier bird
dinewan: emu
dulloora: small grey bird
du-mer: brown pigeon
durroon: night heron
eerin: small grey owl
galah: rose-breasted cockatoo
ga-ra-ga: crane
garaweh: white cockatoo

garganj: chicken hawk
gidgerigar: small parrot
  (budgerigar)
gooboothoo: dove
goola-willeel: topknot pigeon
goolay-yali: pelican
gooloo: magpie
goomble-gubbon: bustard turkey
goonaroo: whistling duck
goonarook: wood duck
goonawarra: swan
goroke: magpie
gowi-nee-bu: robin redbreast
gumalkoolin: willy wagtail
hungappa: crow
iyebana: peewit
jabiru: stork
jenning-gherrie: willy wagtail
jumjum: bellbird
kaar: white cockatoo
kakalan: chicken hawk
kalperri: shoveller duck
kaltee: emu
kaneky: yellow-crested cockatoo
kauert: swan
kearka: bower bird
kelunji: galah
kibulyo: whistler duck
kilkie: water hen
kirli: coot
kirrkie: whistling hawk
kirrpiyirrka: seagull
koa: crow
koiranah: eagle
kolet: dove
konkon: white fish hawk
koodnapina: brown duck
kookaburra: laughing jackass
koolootaroo: magpie lark
koolyn: black swan
koorowera: black diver
koortgang: speckled teal

kora: native companion
korneok: whistling duck
korrorook: stork
koruldambi: white owl
krowalle: blue crane
kuboin: scrub pigeon
kultown: duck
kumalie: small duck
kuracca: crestless white
  cockatoo
kurrowera: shag
kur-ur-rook: native companion
kuyulpi: parrot
lidjet: finch
lirralirra: wren
lowan: mallee fowl
mantaba: bustard
marbangye: black diver
menmenengkuri: martin
millemurro: pelican
miowera: emu
moatah: pigeon
monti: stork
mooaloonyah: pigeon
moongana: white-breasted shag
moogra-ba: black-backed
  magpie
mooregoo: mopoke
mooroocoochin: black swan
mooyi: white cockatoo with
  yellow crest
mugana: willy wagtail
mulduri: magpie
mullian: wedge-tailed eagle
mulundar: swallow
munggi-wurray-mul: seagull
munker: small hawk
murranudda: bustard
murrara: duck
nakkare: musk duck
nangkero: pelican
ndruila: native companion

neenca: sparrow
neeyangarra: eagle
ngerake: teal
ngutam: banana bird
nierrina: hawk
nompie: wedge-tailed eagle
nutam: banana bird
nyungu: Torres Strait pigeon
oorooninannee: grey owl
ooya: quarrion parrot
ooyan: curlew
orra curra: large owl
orrapoora: magpie
padilpa: parrot
paipan: black ibis
panje: black-eared cuckoo
pelde: musk duck
pengana: hawk
pewingi: swamp hawk
pillambi: black cockatoo
pinpi: parrot
pinyali: emu
pipipa: sandpiper
piralko: native companion
pookanah: albatross
poorparta: sparrow hawk
powenyenna: magpie
prolggi: crane (brolga)
punkerri: brown duck
punnamoonta: emu
pupperrimbul: spotted-side finch
puratte: black and white shag
puyulle: emu wren
ragaralti: egret
tallarook: wattle bird
tallawong: bell magpie
tamba: ibis
tappak: bronze-wing pigeon
tarkoori: bittern
tarlarang: red-billed plover
tatea: whistling duck

tchaceroo: magpie
teepookana: kingfisher
tempi: swamp duck
tete: kingfisher
thanpathanpa: snipe
tharalkoo: duck
thowla: spoonbill duck
tiltili: magpie
tityarokan: willy wagtail
tloppere: ibis
toolka: Cape Barren goose
tumakowaller: swan
tuta: parrot
tyepi: quail
tyit: fish hawk
unchurunquar: painted finch
ungjeeburra: crane
urra quarra: grey goose
wahn: crow
wainkan: curlew
wakaje: emu
wakerdi: crow
wanye: mountain duck
warritsha: emu
wata: crow
waukatte: small hawk
wauk-wauk-wa: pigeon
wauwakkeri: grey hawk
waylehmina: swallow
weedah: bower bird
weeloo: curlew
weelya: parakeet
weringerong: lyre bird
wili: pelican
windtha: grey owl
wi-oombeen: robin redbreast
wiwieringgere: native pheasant
woggoon: brush turkey
wollowra: eagle
woltsha: eagle
wonga: pigeon
wonga-wonga: pigeon

woorail: lyre bird
woorawa: wedge-tailed eagle
worippa: storm bird
wornkara: crow
wulde: wedge-tailed eagle
wullaki: black cockatoo
wungghee: owl
wurchiewurchie: white owl
wyralla: black and red cockatoo
yara: seagull
yeranda: black cockatoo
yoldi: black shag
yolla: mutton bird

birth, spirits of: Walla-gudjai-
 wan; Walla-guroon-bu-an
bitch: mooroo
bite: ngolkun; nullgoonie
bittern: tarkoori
black: kineman; kokereka; marroo;
 ourapilla
black-backed magpie: moogra-ba
blackberry, native: mundawora
blackfish: weerap
black snake: ooyu-bu-lui
bladder: kaintyamande; towa
blanket: ititika
blaze (verb): kuntun; towulun
bleat: wirakulun
bleek (fish): mado
bless: kaukau
blind: alknarar-killja; boko;
 milbung; tonde
blood: atnalure; burrabee; gerra;
 kandora; kruwe; kula; midgee;
 yeildo; yerricknar
bloody: kruwalde
blow (verb): kumpun; kurunkun;
 pooney; popa
blowfly: korrumburra; mulgamurra
blue: woorkarrim
blue-gum: eurabbie

blue-tongued lizard: ooboon
blunt: menarte
boat: meralte; warriuka; yuke
boil (noun): engoordna
bone: engwarnar; mulali; neelong;
 pehah; turika
bone, pointing: gooweera; neilyeri
boomerang: kiley; paketye;
 wadna; warroo; yerrawar
boomerang, hunting: maki
boomerang, returning: bargan;
 bubbera
boot: terninyeri; tinabulka
bough: kaki; muldi
bow (verb): meningkundun
bow down: pallarang
bowels: mewe
bower bird: kearka; weedah
box, dwarf: goborro
box tree: angorra; kunakuna
box tree, broad-leaved: bibbil
box tree, flooded: coolabah
box tree, grey-leaved: goolabah
box tree, narrow-leaved: bilkurra
box tree, poplar-leaved: bimbil
boy: apmurika; mutto; ronumdo;
 weehi; wilyango; worlba;
 yerlieyeega
brain: ngurangpar
branch: kandeer
branch, small: ngarlengarl
brand: mah
bread: krepauwe; myhee; nurong;
 wikky
break: luwun; yakalya
breakers: lyeltya
breakfast: peggerambe
break in pieces: tipundun
bream: kooberry; tinuwarre; tukkie
bream, bony: gandjari; wolkolan
breast: ibi; mundi; namma;
 ngumpura

breath: injerima; moldar
breath, offensive: injerima unditta
breathe: narrinyee; winkundun
breathless: piruwallin
bride: carina
bright: ngorkulle; ooliekirra
bring: burreman; morokkun
bring in: yappundun
broke: oltarkim
broken: lulur; yilin
broom wattle: wallowa
brother: binghi; gelar; uckillya
brother, elder: gelane
brother-in-law: ronggi
brother, younger: tarte
bruise (verb): ngultun
brush myrtle: barranduna
brushwood: looranah
buckbush: unmerta
bucket: yirtuggi
budgerigar: betcherrygah; gidgerigar
build: ngarrin
bull oak: belah
bullock: bailaquar; windawityeri
bull roarer: churinga; moiya; pakapaka; gayandi (man's word); gurraymi (woman's word)
bulrush: birwain; wonga
bundle: batturi
burn (verb): kulkun; nyrangkin
bury: grauwun; kralin
bush: see scrub
bush fire: kimba
bush rat: nilee
bustard: goomble-gubbon; mantaba; talkinyeri
busy: burra burra
butcher bird: curriequinquin
butterfish: kundgulde; prandyi
butterfly: bulla bulla; undeelablab

buttock: lewurmi; piningi
by: il
by and by: palli; yun

C

cabbage tree: konda
cake (make of grass seed flour): durri
calf (of leg): kur; pordenpar
call (verb): kaikundun; mearann
camp: baanya; ballarat; koonje; koornkoo; oorla; thulloo-munal; upmurra; uralla
camp (verb): wilpy
camp, deserted: oompi bong
cane grass: appunga
cannibal: bunna
canoe: booltaroo; koorong; likoo; mallana
canoe, bark: goombeelga
Canopus: Womba
cape (point of land): pitye; thrumari
Cape Barren goose: toolka
carp: morwong
carpet shark: goonnear; wobbegong
carpet snake: guridjadu; nurawordubununa
carpet snake, small: dayaminya
carry: thuppun
carry in the arms: pandin
carry off: pintamin
carry on the back: lammin
carry on the shoulder: yityumbarrin
castor oil plant: kudgee
casuarina: see she-oak
cat native: beereek; bukkandi; kinie-ger; ng'rui-moch

cat fish: tandan
cat's cradle (to play): yambalin
catch (verb): argoonie; enamalla;
    kongwak; nanbundun
caterpillar: kelgelli
caught: loorapa; nanbundelin
cause: nungana
cave: narkindie
cave dwelling: gibber-gunyar
caw (verb): wakulun
celebration: yackie
centipede: uaburika
ceremony, initiation: bora
chalk: boolpooli
champion: yoyangamalde
chant: ringbalin
charcoal: yalta
charm (verb): millin; ngadhungi
cheek: make; pertill-lerra
cheerful: narbethong
cherry tree, native: ballat;
    panpande
chest: munde; omenderry; tuldengk
chew: yayin
chicken hawk: garganj; kakalan
chief: rupulle
child: motepa; porle; tyinyeri;
    warooga; umbacoora
childbirth: punden
children: koolyangarra
chin: nootoo; numbe; orodina;
    wacka
chip (verb): drekin; tultun
chisel: binyana
choke: tummun
choose: tambelin
chop (verb): balgoungo
chough (bird): waybung
cinders: keni
circle: arrinyenin; riawunna
circular: larelar
claw: beri; ulbra-cullima

clay: maitlia; tyelde
clay, yellow: wilgee
claypan: alteripa; marloorie
clean: balpewallin; ooliekirra
clean (verb): nyrippin
clematis: minamberang
clever: munkumbole; wi
clever man: koradji; wirinun
clever stick: wimouyan
climb (verb): anjee-malla; caloola;
    pinera
climbing-rat: murra-wunda
cloak: maiyinggar
close (verb): muriltpun
close (adj): ngake
closely woven: kuranye
clothes: see garments
cloud: hotooworry; makoo;
    moorang; okolyer
cloud, white: jombock
cloudy: moki
clover: kuloomba
clover fern: nardoo
club: kanake; kutha; marpanye;
    plongge
club (with head bent at an angle):
    leawill
club (with heavy head): nullanulla
club, double-pointed: mattina
club, fighting: kalduke
club, long: boogoo
club, short: nunkardeol
club, war: waddy
club-headed weapon: boondi
Coalsack, The: Gowa-gay
cobweb: ngilde
cockatiel: ooya; ouyarh
cockatoo: yongana
cockatoo, black: beela, pillambi;
    yeranda; wullaki
cockatoo, black and red: wyralla
cockatoo, crestless white: kuracca

cockatoo parrot: ouyarh
cockatoo, rose-breasted: galah
cockatoo, white: arunta;
  cockalella; garaweh; kaar;
  mooyi
cockatoo, yellow-crested: kaneky
cockle: kuti; tagera
codfish: goodoo
cod, Murray: ponde
cold: appointa; boolea; kilpalie;
  mia; munyertoo; paiala, yake;
  warr-ringa
cold (adj): nruwi
collect: torauwun
come: arndu; burremah; go-oh
come back: yaldeeme; yawoma
come down: yorlun
come here: alleari; kowia; purni
  ngomerna; warrawee
come on: nallak; pichi-malla
command: taiyin
companion: mullaya; nara;
  waminoa
company of people: meli;
  milpara
compassionate: ooyella
conceal: nampulun
conch shell: pundira
conference: yarnirumi
content: noojee
continually: kaldowamp
contrary: ngrelggi
convolvulus: tharook
cook (verb): nammin; prempun
cooked: imbunga
cooking place: myrniong
cool: kilpa; murunkun
coot: kirli
corner: nanowie; ngarti
corpse: utem
cotton bush: mootcha
cough: attong-givilina;

cullgenborn; memerangi;
  ngingeranggi
cough (verb): ngrengkulun
count (verb): tumpun; yelpia
country: mirrow; pimble
cousin: nguyanowi; nonedia; runde
cover (verb): poltha
cover up: turelin
coward: turi kalkir
crab: karlye; krangalang; ugundyi
cramp: plowallin
crane: ga-ra-ga; prolggi;
  ungjeeburra
crane, blue-grey: bootoolga;
  krowalle
crane, white: ragaralti
crayfish: kuniekoondie; meauke
crayfish, small: yabbie
creek: billungah; carroo
creek, small: kurrnung
creek which dries up in summer:
  koorrnong
creep: malkin
crocodile: kambara; kurria
crocodile, freshwater: kena
crocodile, saltwater: pikuwa
crooked: kutkuti; nukuldi; quear;
  ungiverta
cross (bad tempered): kunewallin
  mewe; nyenunkun; talkiwallin
crow (bird): carnka; hungappa;
  koa; wahn; wakerdi; wata;
  wornkara
crow shrike: currawang; tallawong
crows, dance of: kwa
crowd: yunt
crowd (verb): marangane; tokkun;
  yuntuwallin
crush: tipuldun; wurruntun
cry (verb): holanyee; nyerin;
  parpin; yandarlana
cry out: ngangaranden; taikundun

crystals, magic: gubbera
cuckoo, black-eared: panje
cure (verb): ngrallin; nguldun; patyuwarrin
curl (noun): lamaldar
curlew: moolyera; ooyan; wainkan; weeloo
currant, native: karoom; palberry; ungolar
curse (verb): naiyuwun
cut (verb): ampan; coondanie; karrabai; katan; illdo-malla; merippin
cygnet: aroo
cypress pine: jinchilla

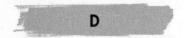

D

dance: corroboree
dance (verb): korobra; ngrilkulun
dance of the crows: kwa
danger: birrie
dark: boolool; ingwa; markrah; moabu; moonga
darkness: ngende; yonguldye
daughter: ngarra
daughter, eldest: pangalarke
dawn: kyeema; trelin ngreye
day: bertana; booroowal; ellhimalla; koora; nunga; pirria; wooremolleen; woorun
day after: kinankurnunk
day before yesterday: kangulun nungge
day, fine: naweenda
daylight: arrah-cardie; awring-gamalla; chintu-ruigin; minkie; woodgera
dead: bong; ill-loong; piruwallin
deaf: irita; plombatye; womba
death: pornurumi

death (spirit that warns of coming): Yowi
death adder: tityowe
death, place of: gunmarl
death wail: goonai
decayed: mirramirildin; pentin
deceit: merrina; wininaru
deceive: winin; yelpulun
decision of the elders in council: tendi
deep: gauware; kummun; quorna; yepperta
delay: garalin; tortuwallin
demon spirit: coocoo-loora; marmoo
deny: nanampundun; tyirpin
depart: nainkulun
depend on: nyerin
depression (forming a natural water hole): gilguy
descend: yorlun
desert: pindan
desert oak: orra-curra; yerra-coppa
desire (verb): duwatyin; parpin mewe
destroy: jindivik; kilkilrarin; ngoweyin
devil: arrunja; brupe; melape
devil, bora: gayandi (man's word); gurraymi (woman's word)
devil-devil: muldarpe; wulgaru
devil, mountain: minn-narie
devil, water: mulloka
devil, whirlwind: wurrawilberoo
devil's bread (fungus): wayway
devils, white: wunda
dew: bananee; ildmurra; pilepi; warroong
diamond-leaved laurel: burrawingie
diarrhoea: prangpin
die: barloona; kukabuka

died: porn il
different: malde
dig: kaltin; towarnie; wyera
digging stick: gunni; wanna
dingo: kua, purnung
dirt: pilbe
dirty: pilbiwallin
disappear: ngokkun
disappeared: tottung
discard: wanta
discussion: yarnirumi; (yarny
  rumour)
disease: yerrakincha
disobedient: plombatye
dissatisfied: nyenkulun
distance, long: beer; bunora
distance, short: kielpa
distant: kummaiyem; kuarun
distinct: narr
district: pimble
dive: tirkundun
diver, black: koorowera;
  marbangye
divide: threttin
divide amongst: peranbim;
  trandararin
doctor: koonkie; kulduke; makga;
  wiwirremalde
dog: irinka; kaddely; madhi; pundi;
  puppa; ucnullya; warrigal;
  warri-kundall; yelga
donkey bird: currawang;
  tallawong
don't: bael
dove: gooboothoo; kolet
down: moru; thanga
down (feathers): ngupe; yunde
down in: loldu
drag: yultun
draw (depict): macooloma
drawing: coolbyngga; wolka
draw towards: yultun

dray: thettherre
dream: aljerer; chooka-chooka;
  pekeri
dream circle: droonoodoo
dream spirit: doowi
dream spirit (of wirinun): mullee
  mullee
dreaming: peggeralin
Dreamland: Alcheringa
dress (verb): yuppundelin
dried: meraldi
drink (verb): alguna; merendamin;
  muttun; quashaunjewma;
  tenjumar
drip (verb): trippin; yanmulun
drive: pildin; waiyin
drive away: trangkin
drop: bartungaran
drop (verb): trippin;
  yanmulun
drought spirit: Yalkara
drowned: nunbalo
drum: plangge
dry: errurraga; kakuri; tyiwi
duck: chippia; kultown; murrara;
  tharalkoo
duck, black: curringa; nakkare;
  punkerri
duck, brown: koodnapina
duck, mountain: wanye
duck, musk: benalla; berallah;
  pelde
duck, shoveller: kalperri
duck, small: kumalie
duck, spoonbill: thowla
duck, swamp: tempi
duck, whistling: chipala;
  goonaroo; kibulyo; korneok;
  tatea
duck, wood: goonarook
dugong: warama
dusk: kaoota; milyaroo

dust: holemunda; mure; oldburra; poi

dwarf box tree: goborro

dying: pornun; pulhiner

E

each: yammiam

each other: mulluna

eagle: bilyarra; koiranah; neeyangarra; wollowra; woltsha

eagle, wedge-tailed: bilyana; mullian; nompie; woorawa; wulde

ear: banarra; beekbeek; thina; thultie; yuri

earth: bimble; munda; pompindho; teangi; tya

earth, red: mooroolbark

east: cocararra; gurra; kumbooran

east wind: gun-ya-mu

eat: mungi; nucka; patter

eating: algooma; nullgoonie; takkin; yayin

echidna: innar-linger; kulai; piggi-billa

echo: iyoura

edge: dilkera

eel: noyang

egg: ambo; booyanga; pateenah; pipi; pompo

egret: ragaralti

eh!: ke

elbow: kuke; neecoo

elder: inkata

elf: nungheenah

ember: kene

embrace (verb): moondani; plunden

emerge: terpulun

empty: maratulde; pek

empty (verb): pekin

emu: boolongena; dinewan; kaltee; miowera; pinyali; punnamoonta; warritsha

emu shoes: kurdaitcha

emu, solitary: gundooi

emu spear: mooroon

emu tail feathers: boobootella; kunarle

emu wren: puyulle

emus, flock of: yallart

end: dalthing; puttheri

enemy: yenamalde

enjoyment: monomeeth

enough: kunye; yikkowun

enter: yappulun

entangle: yenempin

epileptic fit: kungenyeriwallin

equal: mani

escape: tekin

eucalypt: bibbil; coolabah; karri (used only for the W.A. species)

eucalypt, timber of: bangalay (used only for mahogany gum)

evening: kaoota; kongka; pangarinda; tong; wattangger

evening star: marbeangrook

ever: kaldowamp

evergreen: tumbeelluwa

evil: kadaitcha; mungunni

excellent: budgeree; nunkeri

excrement: kunarl kurta

expect: nyerin

expert: munkumbole

extract: yunkundun

exult: nangurwallin

eye: alkingar; cooroo; mea; midna; mil; moonoroo

eyebrow: mague; nanbimba

eyelash: illpilla; nanbean

F

face: petye
fainted: piruwallin
fairy: nungheenah
faith: nglelurumi
fall (verb): ignum; nangalla; ningana
fall backwards: nenengkin
falling: pingkin; wonenie
familiar spirit: yunbeai
fan of emu tail feathers: aroo
far: ku-utyun
far away: katya
farewell: ngoiyun
farm: kulde
fast (speedy): tiwiwarrin
fat: bilpuli; goori; menbi; mooroon; neetee; womma
father: beeyung, cartoo; igeelu; mamma; ngaiyeri; parpinga; uc-neer; yakkoeela
father and child: retulengk
father who has lost a child: randli; waltye
feat: jirrand, wai-i, wauwuawi
feather: entoo; yunde
feathers (down): untita
feathers, band of emu: wurdwurda
feathers, bunch of: kalduke
feathers, emu tail: boobootella; kunarle
feed (verb): munguwun
feel: pleppin
female: booyangan
fern: geewan
fern, clover: nardu
fern tree: kakowera
ferret, native: arutchie
ferret, spotted: kooraltha

fertility, spirit of: Mundook
fester: lanyalin
fetch: kldeimindin
feud: dullay-mullay-lunna
few: lakebi; maltaiar
fiercely: murri-cooler
fig: hill-lee; ngarningi
fig, blue: callangun
fig tree: natan; taree
fig tree, rough-leaved: balemo
fight: yoyangi
fight (verb): durellie; goonder-rah; mendin; yarrak
fighting stick: worraworra
fill (a hole): thungana
fin: lidjet; manar; wunba
finch, painted: unchurunqua
finch, spotted-sided: pupperrimbul
find: pingyin
finger: illcha; kerlpra; murra; punjil
fingernail: geppmorra; melinya; perar
finish: chenka; dalthing; moodunna; nguldin; pekin
fire: booreah; kudla; nandalie; warroo; wi; wi-buloo; wur
fire, bush: kimba
fire, large: orucknurra
fire, small: maka
fireplace: goorung
firestick: kene; tauwangi
fire-walking: weeriga
firewood: wiena
firework: poolooloomee
firm: pritye
first: kangulandai
fish: errabunga; kooya; mame; wunta
fish (verb): werguttulun; werkin

FISH and CRUSTACEANS:

akama: whale
anka: barramundi
bangnalla: golden perch
barramundi: giant perch
culma: a spiny fish
dyintan: nail fish
gandjari: bony bream
goodoo: codfish
ita: swamp fish
kaandha: whale
karlye: crab
kondarle: whale
kongoola: river fish
kooberry: bidyan ruffe or silver perch
koo-ee-lung: porpoise
kringyang: sand mullet
kunara: tiger shark
kundgulde: butterfish
kyena: baracoota
lerunna: flounder
luderick: black fish
mado: bleek or trumpeter fish
mallowe: Murray mouth salmon
maray: pilchard
meauke: crayfish
miitinta: sea turtle
morwong: jackass fish
nannygai: redfish
ngarakkani: shark
noyang: eel
otama: porpoise
pomeri: mud-fish
ponde: Murray cod
prandyi: butterfish
puntyaiya: swamp turtle
tandan: cat-fish
tarki: perch
tealedyan: shark
tinuwarre: bream
trata: knight-fish
tukkeri: flat, silvery fish
tukkie: bream
tupong: marble-fish
tyeli: swamp fish
ugundyi: crab
umpara: stingray
warama: dugong
weerap: blackfish
welappe: mullet
wi: a small fish
wirralee: gin-fish
wobbegong: carpet shark; snapper
wolkolan: bony bream
wollomai: snapper
yabbie: small crayfish
yauoanggi: porpoise

fish hawk: tyit
fish hawk, white: konkon
fishing line: nunggi; perlka
fishing net: kulkulook
fish trap: barameda
fist-fighting: nguldunguldelin
five: kuk kuk ki; ngerla; yeyakki
flame: aloripma; color; leripma; ngorkulli
flap (verb): mapa
flat: nanarlin; wurrook
flathead, freshwater: tupong
flea: tittadi
flee: nginbundim
flesh: kooka; manba; ngulde
flick: pernmin
flock: malyar
flood: koorpa
flood water on polygonum flats: warrambool
flounder: lerunna
flour: nunungki

flow (verb): adnamira; pombulun; raiaralin
flower: patya; thiewie
flowers, place of: girraween
flute: ulpirra
fly (insect): bun-yal; mongana; tyilye; yumbera
fly (verb): koomeela; ngarntin
fly, march: ill-lulta
flying fox: wuka
flying squirrel: berring; buggoo; butterga; mangaroo; pongo; tuan
fog: ubeeterra
foliage: muldi
follow: warreyin
fondle: tunkun
food: diale; mai; myrna
food (fruit and vegetable): mai; maiye; ngune
food, animal: kooka; mam; ngulde
food bag: koorngoo
food, bush: rarkee; undarnga
food for a journey: potyanambe
foolish: bailpulun
foot: chinna; jenoong; mintchie; mundooie; thina
footprint: geenong; tshina
for: ambe; arami
ford: penghanah
forehead: bruye; nullar; rogoona
forehead band: garbai
foreign: malde
foreigner: yammin uwar korn
forequarter: tuldi
forest, dense: kiambram
forget: bailpulun; tainpulun
four: koorunga; wima
friend: mullaya; ngaitye; runde; waminda; wirake
frighten: nganden

frightened: hatarear-amalla; turlin
frightening: thrunkun; turlemindin
frog: bun-yun bun-yun; menperre; tata; tiddalick; yuaia
frog, bull: tuki
frog, climbing: tendu
frog, green: withinka
from: anyir
frost: parattah; peti
froth: kulde
frown: indarnie; pilkundun
fruit: nunungki
fuel: ooeena
full: yalkin
fun: borak
fungus (devil's bread): wayway
fur: inntoo; yunde
future: paldi; yun

G

galah: kelunji
galaxy: warring
game, wild: kembla
games: riawena
gap: undia
garment: kambie
garment (cloak): maiyinggar
garment (woman's skirt): goomilla
garment, skin: poltha
garments: mundarra
gently: mant
geranium: iperta
get: morokkun
get inside: thopramolla
get on: thopramolla
get up: akamarei
ghost: moma; onya; wunda
ghost, female: pino
gin fish: wirralee
girdle: see belt

girl: bami; birra-li; cue-on-
   buntor; lowana; unkeegeega;
   whitkitha
girl, adolescent: aragoodgeawonga; quei-marla;
   wirreebeeun
girl, big: quei-marla; yartuwe
girl, little: cue-on-mema; quei
give: antye; gnoka; pempin;
   ungooroo; warrina; youhi
glad: carbethon; kunthun
gladness: kunthuld
go: loru; ngomerna; ngowalle;
   padewer; yan
go!: ngowalour
go away: brimhillah; yinbaikulun
go away!: taiyin; thrunkkun
go back: colba; collumbum
go before: ngunkurawallin
go down: birrama; loldu; moru
go on: albye; byenie
go up: gulle
goanna: adjunepa; awadabir;
   beewee; googarh; hurramira;
   mungoon-gali; tatya; weenduga
goanna, short-tailed: klare;
   munnari
**goanna, yellow and brown
   striped:** perindi
goblin: wullundigong
gold: karakara
golden perch: bangnalla
good: boorala; budgeree;
   goorunna; gubba; kandelka;
   nunkeri; yetto
good, being: nunkowallin
goose, Cape Barren: toolka
gooseberry, native: bookabooda
goose, grey: urra-quarra
gorge: undia
grand-child (on father's side):
   maiyarare

grand-child (on mother's side):
   bakkare
grandfather: nerbungeron;
   ngaityapalle; pola; tipi; ulwai
grandmother: bargi
grandmother (paternal):
   maiyanowe
grandmother (maternal):
   bakkano
grass: kindyerra; korra; narmar;
   putta; wongoonoo
grass, good: tour-ur-rong
grasshopper: chintillga; ungee-
   gungee
grass, rat-tail: jil-crow-a-berry
grass seed: doonbur
grass for thatching: illpellpa
grass shelter: nunnoo
grass tree: karwin; nglaiye
grass, wire: elilger
grassy: kilto
gravel: lilla
gravel, brown: coorang
great: battur; cabon; matong;
   murna
greedy: pele; pulkeri
green: iterika; ngthummulun;
   norabeetya; thumelin; worooa
grey: kenkulun
grey-haired: kenkank
grind: ngenempin
grindstone (for grinding grass
   seed): dayoorl; doori
ground: aka; tuni; yerilla
ground, level: wirrelyerna
ground, parched: klallin ruwe
ground, soft: ditta
ground, stony: mrangalli
grow: kringgun
growl: ngrakkuwallin
grub: nuttoo; poontee; yulumara
grub, edible: witchetty

grub, edible (found in banksia):
pellati
guard: tupun; turuwun
guilty: ngommi
guilty of murder: malpuri
gully: dheran
gum, edible: tangari
gum of pine or gumtree:
pitchingga
gum leaf: ghera
gum, river red: yarrah
gum, slaty-: arangnulla
gum, tuart: tooart
gum, wandoo: wandoo
gumtree: bael-bael; bernaroo;
choota; heeterra
gumtree, blue: ballook
gumtree, large: waranyukbeal
gumtree, red: wuri
gumtree, white: tooart; wandoo
gun: pandappure; popogina

H

hailstones: moogaray; paldharar
hair: alta; arkoola; burlkie;
dhilla; hooray; kagailya;
nguroo; yaran
hair, grey: kuna
half: mirimp; ngalluk; oticha
hand: atnitta; ilchar; mah; murra;
turni
hand, left: warrame
hand, right: nunkeri-mari;
purrinunggi
handsome: nunkeri
hang: wallin
happy: yackatoon
hard: piltengi
hare: wirlpa
hat: morquita

hatchet: drekurmi
hate: paiyin
have: annin; watyin
hawk: biaga; nierrina; pengana
hawk, chicken: garganj; kakalan
hawk, grey: wauwakkeri
hawk, orange-speckled: berigora
hawk, small: munker, waukatte
hawk, swamp: pewingi
hawk, whistling: kirrkie
he: atye; ba; kitye; yato; yetni
head: cobbra; cutta; kokora;
konkaer kukaa; kurle; therto
headband (painted white): nulu-
gail
head-dress: oogee
heal: tumbetin
healthy: nguldun
heap: batturi
heap up: pokkoremin
hear: coleenie; kungun; ungroo;
yuri
heart: gootagoodo; ngele;
otorkweta; panda
heat: goornan; kiata; pukara;
woolta
heaven: booloot; bullima
heavens: see sky
heavy: bunckanee; enborra;
poonta; thackory
heel: moocoo; retyinne
help carry a load: kalparrin
here: alye; kalyan; nia
heron, night: durroon
hiccough: tummun
hidden: nammuldi
hide: nampulun
hide-and-seek: wahgoo
high: booral; neerim; warre
hill: banool; deetoo;
poymalangta; purri
hill, wooded: moliagulk

hillside: warraroong
hills, many: callemondah
him: ityan; kin; noonga
hip: alknarlee; cullebee; pilpati
his: kinauwe; yato
hit: balka; battana; poonganyee
hold: mama; morokkun;
    taldumbarrin; wettinnie
hold on: wonnewarra
hole: auwa; chookola; gnamma;
    iperta; merke; pinah; yeppa
hole, deep: mooroopna
hole in the ground: minga;
    nerntulya
hole in the side: namero pinah
hole, large: perki
hole, small: merki
holiday: pink-hi
honey: kurmoonah; pinyatowe
honey-ant: yarumpah
honeysuckle: warrah; woorak
honeysuckle tree: lakkari
hoof: inger
hope (verb): wruwallin
horn, bullock's: yourula
horse: inger-godill; yarraman
horse, wild: brumby
hot: comebunyee; kaloola;
    ottinna; wappilka
house (see also hut): taldumande
how: mengye; yarild
howl (of wind—verb): tullun
howl (dog—verb): lokulun
hunger: ringmail
hungry: hungiaquar; unmaturra;
    yeyauwe
hunt (noun): konkonbah
hunt (verb): thumpun
hunter: mundurra
hunting ground: noorumba
hurry (verb): murrunmil;
    tyiwewar; wutherama

hurt (verb): partin; wirin
husband: coorie; lielu; murta;
    napalle
hut: hillta; mia-mia; ngura; oorla;
    wiltja; wurley
hut, bark: dardur; gunyah;
    humpy
hut, grass: nunnoo

I: nappa; ngai-i; niu
ibis: paipan; tamba; tloppere
ice: ellulger; plomare; wolka
if: ungun
iguana: see goanna
ill (illness): minga; wirin
immediately: hikkai; karlo
infant: kelgalli; malagenna;
    milyali; partumbe
inform: rammin; tingowun
initiation ceremony: bora;
    engwura
insect: bulga-nunnoo; mongana;
    teeta

INSECTS etc.:

arrama: louse
atnaterta: scorpion
bogong: edible grey moth
boongurr: water beetle
brupe: spider
bun-yal: fly
carltooka: bulldog ant
chintillga: grasshopper
chumbee: torpedo bug
cooba: black stingless bee
ill-lulta: march fly

kelgelli: caterpillar
koongun: scorpion
korrumburra: blowfly
kotbityerowe: bull ant
kunabinjelu: mosquito
kundy: mosquito
kuyan: honey bee
mako: edible wood grub
minga: small black ant
mirta: white ant
mongana: fly
mulgamurra: blowfly
murga muggai: trapdoor
    spider
murule: mosquito
nalgarmyeri: bull ant
nanarinyeri: sandfly
neanye: fly
nokarugge: locust
noora-gogo: orange and blue
    beetle
nuttoo: grub
odunepa: white ant
ollo: brown bee
oomborra: maggot
ouratita: black beetle
pellati: edible grub
petachall-lily: scorpion
pintapinta: moth
poontee: grub
prilde: ant
teeta: ant
tittadi: flea
tokiejonburnba: bulldog ant
tunkeri: louse
tyilye: fly, maggot
uaburika: centipede
undee-lablab: butterfly
undeneya: wasp
ungee-gungee: grasshopper
unya: louse
unwinnia: mosquito

uwoppa: spider
warra-nunna: bee
warroo-culla: moth
wirpa: ant
witchetty: edible grub
wonka: spider
yarumpah: honey-ant
yeramba: sugar-ant
yerra: ant
yulu-mara: grub
yumbera: fly

inside: maremuntunt
intelligible: narr
intestines: tipi
into: angk
ironbark, narrow-leaved:
    parragilga
ironbark tree: odenpa
is: el
island: kallakkure; karte;
    thankomalara
it: ba; kitye; yetni
itch (noun): wirrullummi
itch (verb): kirkuwe; kuwulun

J

jackass fish: morwong
jackass, laughing: goo-goor-
    gaga; kookaburra
jealous: kraiyelin; toorange
jealousy: biminya
jew lizard: armoolya; kunnie
joint: tunggar
joke (verb): rumalduwallin
joy: kunthuld
joyful: kindilan
jump (verb): taitpullun; walla
jump quickly: walla-walla

K

kangaroo: arinya; arrurra;
bamburr; bohra; boolgana;
boondar; koola; koongarra;
marloo; munthu; woora
kangaroo apple: gunyang
kangaroo, large: wallaroo
kangaroo rat: aloota; goonur;
millia; potoroo; purtia
kangaroo, short-legged:
wurgulin
kangaroo skin: cudgewong
kangaroo skin bag: kumbi
kangaroo, small: wallaby
keep: daiyuwun
kelp: koonthooi
kick (verb): atninebeemalla;
cundoonie; illgulldenem;
ngultun
kidney: purri; therna-perty
kidney fat: yuntheyunthe
kill: mempin; poonganyee;
pornumindin
kindle: ngungyen
kingfisher: berrimilla; boondoon;
teepookana; tete
kiss: kunden; moinpunden;
neenjeweny; ol-dorry-e-way;
tshuppana
knee: jirriman; murtee; turtangi
kneel: luwun-turtangk; umbee-
leedin-gorra; wakkin-turtangk
knife: drekurmi
knife, stone: muggil; womba
knight-fish: trata
knock: ngurunguldun
knot: kerlpa; tirkeri
know: nglelin
koala: banjora; boorbee;
burrendong; carbora;
coolabun; koala; koob-bor;
kulla; kur-bo-roo; nargoon;
nurrumpi; wirngill; yarri
kurrajong tree: nonga
kurrajong tree bark: mooroomi
kurrajong trees, many:
toolangatta

L

lagoon: beeree
lagoon, freshwater: kolora
lake: boloke; marloorie-buntor;
mungkule
lake, brackish: keilambete
lament (verb): plowallin
lame: muntye; turokkul
land: pelepe; ruwe; thockyar;
yerta
land, area of: panitya
land beyond the sky: Ungant;
Barachi
landing place: krambruk
language: kalde; tunggarar
languid: munainpulun
large: cabon; grauwe
larger: grauwe ru
lark, magpie: koolootaroo
last (final): karlowan atye;
ngurukuwarrin
laugh (verb): incarnie; kangkin;
kinedana; kinka; kinkuna
laugh at: kanggen
laughing jackass: goo-goor-gaga;
kookaburra
laughter: karbeethong
laurel, diamond-leaved:
burrawingie
lay eggs: pindattulun
lazy: etrakee; hetrala; putta
lead (verb): wrendu; yultun

leaf: baibaiye; illperipa; kirra; palpera

leaf, gum: ghera

leaf, palm: tuta

leak: pombulun

lean on: tauwin

leave (verb): imbye; jeetho; nemmin

leave off: nemmin

leaves: muldi

leech: manninkki; uwa

leg: karaka; mundooie; tarrukengk; wittha

legends: woggheeguy

let out: adaka-palai

lick: arntuney; timpin

lie (falsehood): purragia

lie down: ngar-binya; tantin; woonah; yuppun

life: tumpinyeri

lift: meya; plunden; preppin; walpa

light (adj): dalyo; kaikai

light (noun): baringa; burra; nunkalowe; pitura

light (verb): ngungyen

light, rays of: tyelyerar

lightning: doon-gara; nalin; nalurmi; pinpan

lightning man: Mamaragan

like (similar): luk; nglalin

like (verb): pornun

lime: bulpuli

limestone: drik-drik; marti

limpet: banawara

line: pitti

linger: ngaralin

lip: arrie-enpa; munengk

liquid: pan

listen: nurrungar

listen!: kung our

little: mije; muralappi; narang

live (verb): numberleya; tumbe

live at a place: yallambee

lively: narbeethong

liver: allue; kalkerri; yerhillga

lizard: kendi; lurki

lizard, barking: coorabin; wallubarl

lizard, blue-tongued: ooboon; wala

lizard, jew: armoolya; kunnie

lizard, large: elloi-jerra; punka

lizard, prickly: kami

lizard, red: gudda

lizard, red prickly: oola

lizard, sand: goolee

lizard, small prickly: beereeun

lizard, wood: bu-maya-mul

locust: nokarugge

log: ngarari

long: gora; mahn; neerim; wattora

long ago: ngulli

long time: arr-reedy

long way: ill-lamanoo; wernma

look: nokuna; tumaquoi

look for: tuyulawarrin

look out: nak our; nunghungee

look round: nanauwun; willkilla

loose: yankulun

lose: jindivik

loud: tyiwewar

louse: arrama; tunkeri; unya

love: wombalano; yooralla

love (verb): kungkungullun; pornun; woorinyan; yoorami; yoorana

love, will: yooralanni

loved: kungkungundun

low (verb): morallie

lungs: pelberrimunt

lying: winin; yelpulun

lying on the back: korowalkin

lyre bird: bulln-bulln;
weringerong; woorail

M

mad: pilyaulun; womba
Magellan Clouds: prolggi;
wurrawilberoo
maggot: oomborra; tyilye
magic, black: ungwilla
magic stones: gubbera
magpie: gooloo; goroke;
mulduri; orrapoora; powenyenna; tchaceroo
magpie, bell or **black:**
currawang; tallawong
magpie, black-backed: moogra-
ba
magpie lark: koolootaroo
mahogany, swamp or **bastard:**
jarrah
mahogany tree: coo-in-new
make: ngarrin; pinjaroo; winmin
mallee fowl: lowan; woggoon
man: atwa; bartoo; korne; kurda;
malie; naroa-mine; yerdlee
man and wife: nandroya
man, married: napowatyeri
man, old: bartoo-gilbee; pinaroo;
wherto
man, unmarried: yan yean
man, white: amerjig
man, young: kaingani; oolyarra;
taldree
mangrove: egaie; korpie
mangrove, red: kowinka
manhood: thalera
manhood, girdle of: bor
manna (exudation from tree):
buumbuul; wahler
manna (secretion of insect): lerp

many: multuwallin; murna;
murri; ngruwar
many times: ngurintand
marble-fish: tupong
march fly: ill-lulta
mark: minar
married man: napowatyeri
married woman: hokarra
marrow: bailpuli
marry: napwallin
Mars: gwai-billah
martin: menmenengkuri
mat: punde; tullingapperi; yallane
mate: kuldi; mullaya; wiraki
mating fever: unja
me: an; guana; natoah; ngan;
ngottha; nihooloo
mean: thirti
meat: barru; minna
meat, raw: tumbe an ngulde
medicine: ungwarlyer
medicine man: boyla: coradji;
kobi; wirinun
meet: thuldun; uwan
melt: yalkundun
mesh: mea
messenger: brigge
messmate tree: kampa
midday: gauwel; kalkree;
kardingoola; warridanga
midden, shell: mirnyong
middle: tunte
middle one: tarrinyeri
midnight: odneler
milk: ngumperi; woolladgeilkna
Milky Way: warrambool
mine: atchina; guie; mirambeek;
ngaitshi
mirage: eer-dher; hipmilta
miserable: talkiwallin
mist: boorrang; injeer-mayjeer;
jombok; pouraller

mistletoe: bahn
mix: yultuwarrin
mock: kabbulun; kappin
monster: bunyip; eer-moon-an; nulu-yoon-du
monster with two toes: eleanba wunda
moon: bahloo; bigha; etninja; merrican-kein; peer; pitoa
moon god: Bahloo
moon, new: ingitja
moonlight: goolara; nulgerong
mopoke: bingami; boobook; mooregoo
more: kutsha; nerntoma; owadema
more, much: ngruinyerar
Moreton Bay ash: ilumba
morning: barperipna; nooroobunda
morning, early: tong kongka
morning star: mullian-ga; nunkumbil
mosquito: kunabinjelu; kundy; murule; uwinnia
moth: pintapinta; warrooculla
moth, edible grey: bogong
mother: babaneek; gunee; igera; meer; namarra; numba-di; wia; yackhoo; yanga
mother and child: rattulengk
mother-in-law: karinye; nielongan
motherless: kulgutye
mother who has lost child: wirratye
mountain: barree; ngurle
mountain ash: warreah
mountain devil (a spiny lizard): ming-ari; min-jin; minn-narie; nai-ari
mountain, high: wollumbin

mountain range: pullybuntor
mouse: koonappoo; pundeol
moustache: muninyeri
mouth: arrakata; mumnunah; nimi; tar; thunbira; tore; yelka
move: ellin; ngoppun
much: murna; ngruwar; waycoot
much, too: multuwarrin
mud: ditter; menengi
mud-fish: pomeri
mud-shell: kumala
mullet: welappe
mullet, sand: kringyang
murder, guilty of: malpuri
Murray cod: ponde
muscle: ngulde
mushroom: bambra; parrumbal; wanappe
musical instrument: didjeridoo
musk duck: benalla; berallah; pelde
mussel: lokure; munggi; tyelokuri; yea
mutton bird: yolla
my: nganauwe
myall, weeping: boree
myrtle bush: barranduna
myself: kooronya**

N

nail: milltee
nail-fish: dyintan
naked: merate; palthawangalana
name: arrainya; mitye; nakame
name (verb): krunkun
narrow: tokorauwe
native or **native born:** myee
native companion: brolga; kora; kur-ur-rook; ndruila
nautilus: wietatenana

navel: bullyee; inyeppa
near: munggai; tapangk
near me: alyenik; hik alye
near you: tapangk
neck: arruleta; erringer; hontee;
  kure
necklace: intinne
necklace, reed: tarrgoorn
needlebush: binga-wingul
neighbour: tauel
nest: malunna; ngauandi; oorla;
  worda
nest, bees': calimpa
net (verb): ngerin; tuldin
net, fishing: kulkulook; ngeri;
  puntaman
nettle, giant; irtaie
never: tarnalo
new: mokari; ooliekirra
'new chum': munjong; myall
night: biangri; bolool; maltthi;
  mundil; nuta; wiltcha
night heron: durroon
night owl: bulooral
nipple: ngumperi
no: baal; bael; illa-illa; jitcha;
  mopa; mukka; wahl; weumpa
no!: tauo
no good: arcoona; quear
noise, to make a: turrammelin
noisy, to be: panelgorana
none: nowaly; wee-ar
noon: kardingoola
north: alinjarra; gurburra;
  walkandi
north-west wind: mundewudda
north wind: douran douran
nose: allar; ammoula; mendolo;
  mudla
nostril: allang-goola; olltoo
not: bael; illa-illa; nowaiy; tarno;
  tauo

nothing: nowaiy ellin; thundarta
now: au
nurse (verb): plunden; tunkun
nut tree: burrawang

O

oak, desert: orra-curra; yerra-
  coppa
obtain: morokkun
ocean: panamuna
ochre, red: korralo; olba; werrup
offended: nyenunkun
offspring: milyali tinyeri
often: ngurintand
oh!: yakkai
old: coolbaroo; kaldowinyeri;
  ranwul; yande
old man: bartoo-gilbee; pinaroo;
  wherto
old woman: koon-ja-gilbee;
  meetawarri
one: cooma; goochagoora;
  tarlina; yammalaitye
open: pintannie
open (verb): ngiralin; ngramin
open!: ngramal
opening: tari
opossum: see possum
orange (colour): milkurli
orange-speckled hawk: berigora
orange tree, native: bingelima;
  bumble; umbellditta
Orion's belt: amayworra
ornament, string: mundamunda
orphan: kukathe
other: kangulun; yam
our: ngurnauwe
ours: nindethana
ourselves: moonthalie
outside: itye; ngurukwar

oven: goorung; krugapupe; purni
oven, prepare an: prumpun
overcome: wityungyin
overflow: raiaralin
over there: warra
overthrow: pinggen
overturned: ngerakowen
owl (see also mopoke):
  wungghee
owl, grey: ooroowinannee
owl, large: orra curra
owl, night: bulooral
owl, small grey: eerin; windtha
owl, white: koruldambi;
  wurchiewurchie
oyster: koonwarra; wara; yerlata

P

paddle (verb): ngibalin
paddymelon: mai-ra
pain: minga; wiwirri
paint (verb): macooloma
painted finch: unchurunqua
painting: coolbyngga; wolka
pair: ninkaiengk
palm, feathery-leaved: bangalow
palm leaf: tuta
pandanus: kuntyan
pant: ngrengkulun; nyerpulun;
  wankin mewe
paper-bark: see tea-tree
parakeet: weelya
parrot: bartill; kuyulpi; padilpa;
  pinpi; tuta
parrot, crimson-wing: billai
parrot, green: bullai bullai
parrot, quarrion: ooya
parrot, small (budgerigar):
  gidgerigar
part (verb): threttin

passion: ngrakkuwallin
pass (verb): ngauwun
path: yarluke
pause (verb): cooragook
pea, Sturt's desert: meekyluka
peace: gwandalan; thoomee
  yant
peace-maker: mereki
peach tree, native: quandong
pear tree, native: thoopara
pearl shell: namaga
pebble: moomowroong
peel (verb): wurtun
peewit: burrengeen; iyebana
pelican: booran; goolay-yali;
  millemurro; nangkero; wili
pendant: wallin
penis: carloo; menane
people: narrinyeri
pepper, native: mao-warang
perch (fish): tarki
perch, giant: barramundi
perch, golden: bangnalla
perch, silver: kooberry
perch, trumpeter: mado
periwinkle: moondara
permanent: killara
persuade: nanampundun
pheasant, native: lowan;
  wiwieringgere
pick up: makkin; mama;
  mungeenie; pintyin
pick out: pindyin
piece, small: narteol
pieces: pruwuttar
pied crow shrike: tchaceroo
pierce: tappin
pigeon: moatah; mooaloonyah;
  wauk-wauk-wa; wonga;
  wonga-wonga
pigeon, bronze-wing: tappak
pigeon, brown: du-mer

pigeon, scrub: kuboin
pigeon, topknot: goola-willeel
pigeon, Torres strait: nyungu
pigface (plant): canajong;
  karkalla
pigweed root: kunnan-beili
pilchard: maray
pillow: kalbe
pinch (verb): minntin; puttun;
  tokkun
pine, cypress: jinchilla
pines, place of: carawatha
pine tree: bunya-bunya; maroo;
  maroong; mowantyi; pimpala;
  pyingerra
pipeclay: bulpuli; durdaak;
  marloo
pity (verb): wanbin
place (noun): wal
place (verb): throttun; yuppun
plain: arcurrata; kaikai; maneroo;
  woorak
plain, sandy: koolena
plain surrounded by forest:
  koyuga
plant (verb): nompulun; rata

PLANTS

appung: cane grass
aquaie: pink water-lily
arika: small blue water-lily
arnurna: blue water-lily
bahlaka: saltbush
bambra: mushroom
binga-wingul: needlebush
birwain: bulrush
bookabooda: native
  gooseberry
boringkoot: native raspberry
canajong: pigface
chilla: poison bush

chucky-chucky: wax cluster
  berry
elilger: wire grass
erladgeer: yam
evrah: a drooping shrub
geewan: common fern
goberta: plum bush
goborro: dwarf box
gunyang: kangaroo apple
gweebet: creeper with edible
  fruit
honggar: reed
iperta: geranium
irriakura: edible tuber
irtaie: giant nettle
ita: scrub
iyouta: spinifex
jil-crow-a-berry: rat-tail grass
kanpuka: white water-lily
kaooroo: water-lily
karagata: umbrella bush
karoom: native currant
kindyerra: grass
kineyah: rice
kodala: reed
koonthooi: kelp
korpi: mangrove
korra: grass
kudgee: castor oil plant
kuloomba: native clover
kuntyari: plant with edible
  leaves
kurrajong: kurrajong tree
kurrawan: reed
loombrak: water grass
looranah: brushwood
mai-ra: paddy-melon
mallee: scrub of dwarf
  eucalypts
meekyluka: Sturt's desert pea
minamberang: clematis
mirria: polygonum shrub

mootcha: native cotton bush
mulwala: possum grass
mundawora: native blackberry
murr-nong: plant with edible tuber; yam
nardoo: clover fern
naretha: salt bush
narmar: grass
omil-dadgee: bamboo; large reed
palberry: native currant
parrumbal: mushroom
pitchery: plant with narcotic leaves
putta: grass
talga: sow thistle
tallerk: thistle
thalaak: sow thistle
tharook: convolvulus
uc-aliera: reed
ungarunya: rush
ungolar: native currant
unmerta: buckbush
wanappe: mushroom
warrah: honeysuckle
watye: polygonum shrub
wayway: devil's bread fungus
wididna: truffle
wiinki: arrowroot
wonga: bulrush
wongoonoo: grass
woorak: honeysuckle
wotiya: yam
yallaban: native raspberry
yerrear: saltbush

platypus: baarlijan; gayadari; theen-who-ween
play (verb): era cunalerme; nanyima; tunkuwallin
pleasant: murrumbung
pleasant place: elouera

Pleiades, The: maya-mayi
plentiful: woowookarung
plenty: curbarra; kowa; marandoo; moona
plenty, place of: bullarrto
plover, red-billed: tarlarang
pluck: thrintin
pluck feathers: teriltin
plucked: takkure
plum bush: goberta
plum tree, native: boomarrah; goberta
point (noun): padmuri
pointed: padmurwallin
pointing bone: gooweera; neilyeri
poison bush: chilla
poison stick: toorli
poke: tolkun
polygonum shrub: mirria; watye
pool: billabong; mianameena
pool with reeds: mallanbool
poor: woomelang
porcupine: see echidna
porpoise: koo-ee-lung; otama; ya uoanggi
portion, small: minti
possessions: maiyinggar
possum: kulan; leena; moodai; porlta; tarmaroo; wyehoota; yarraringy
possum, black-tailed: banya
possum grass: mulwala
possum, ring-tailed: wongguri
pour: raiaramin; yaramin
pour water into a vessel: thickathickana
prayer: marmingatha
prepare: anangkwarrin
press (verb): poroany
press heavily: wityungyin
pretence: merrina

pretty: nunkeri
prickle: chillkalla; licka
prickly lizard, red: oola
prickly lizard, small: beereeum
promise (verb): ngoiyir
protect: koolkuna
proud: plaityinggin
pull (verb): hetarracadin;
    werendun; wonthaggi
puppy: wumbi
pursue: prildin
pus: thuldi
push (verb): pinbittulun; pinpin
put: pinpin
put down: throttun
put together: tanpundun; tulgeen

Q

quail: beereegan; burrandool;
    tyepi
quarrel (verb): yabm-irriti
quarrion parrot: ooya
quartz: allirra
quick: burra burra, mickie;
    murinmelin; nooroo; tiewiwar
quiet: gwandalan; tortuwallin;
    weeronga; wepe

R

rage: ngraldi
rain: allabuckinee; chillberto;
    eehu; mangnoo; mincarlie;
    wainbaru
rain (verb): cobbycoononyee;
    cobbyworrall; quashaundema
rain, much: trawalla
rain-bird: boogoo-doo-ga-da
rainbow: koninderie; ooranye;

wee-y-teena; yulu-wirree
rainbow snake: Yurlunggur
rain-making, stone for:
    oodoolay
raise: preppin
raspberry, native: boringkoot;
    yallaban
rat: cowirrie; ertargwar; umorra
rat, bandicoot: bilba
rat, bush: nilee
rat, climbing: murra-wunda
rat, kangaroo: aloota; goonur;
    millia; potoroo; purtia
rat, large: qualpar
rat, long-snouted: pulyara
rat, water: biggoon; goomai;
    rekaldi
rat-tail grass: jil-crow-a-berry
raw: erlicha; tumbi
receive: pultin
recline: allambee
red: beebeethung; gwai; itichika;
    prolin
redbreast, robin: gwai-nee-bu
red pigment: kuging-cudgen
reed: hong-gar; kodala;
    kurrawan; uc-aliebra
reed, large: omildadgee
refuse (verb): petin; wenkin
rejoice: tunthun
relative: kurnkuni; morannie
remain: allambee; auminthina
remains: nemmuran;
    yertauwullar
remember: ngullun
repose: eumina

REPTILES (see also snakes):

adjunepa: goanna
armoolya: jew lizard
awadabir: goanna

beereeun: small prickly lizard
beewee: goanna
binking: turtle
bu-maya-mul: wood lizard
bun-yun bun-yun: frog
coorabin: barking lizard
elloi-jerra: large lizard
garbarli: shingleback
googarh: goanna
goolee: sand lizard
guddha: red lizard
hurramira: goanna
kambara: crocodile
kami: prickly lizard
kena: freshwater crocodile
kendi: lizard
kinkindele: tortoise; turtle
klare: short-tailed goanna
kunnie: jew lizard
kurria: crocodile
lurki: lizard
menperre: frog
ming-ari: mountain devil
minjin: mountain devil
minn-narie: mountain devil
mungoon-garli: goanna
munnarie: short-tailed goanna
nai-ari: mountain devil
ooboon: blue-tongued lizard
oola: red prickly lizard
perindi: yellow and brown striped goanna
pikuwa: saltwater crocodile
punka: large lizard
tata: frog
tatya: goanna
tendu: climbing frog
thidnamura: toad
tiddalick: frog
tuki: bull-frog
wala: blue-tongued lizard
wallu-barl: barking lizard

wangarang: tortoise
warka: tortoise
wayamba: turtle
wayembeh: tortoise
weenduga: goanna
withinka: green frog
yuaia: frog

resemble: nglalin
resin: giddie
rest (verb): gwandalan; kunden
resting place: weeroona
return: ngaiambin
rib: prewarrar; wolter
rice: kineyah; tyilyi
ridge, sand: urdera
ridge, stony: morilla
right: nunkeri
right hand: nunkeri-mari
ring: illyer-manda
ringlet: poenghana
rise (verb): doonkami; prakkin; prakour
river: balun; billa; bindaree; kur; lerra; milloo
river bend: nerreman
river red gum tree: yarrah
river, rocky: corowa
river, winding: nambucca
road: uworra; yutthero
robin redbreast: gwai-nee-bu
rock: gibber; gnamma; marti
rock shelter: gibber-gunyah
roll (verb): menamenakarin
root: itickera; tipi; werrook
root, pigweed: kunnan-beili
root, tree: kahar; meralki
root, young (of reeds): lintyeri
rope: kandari; nunggi
rose-breasted cockatoo: galah
rosewood tree: boodha
rot (verb): pultuwarrin

rotten: mirramerildin; rorari
rough: wirritin
round: larelar
round about: laldilald
rub: kilkilyalin; partin
rug, possum skin: pirriwee
run: klein; mana; moa; unti
run about: likkaldin
run away: nginbundun
rush: ungarunya

S

saliva: kulde
salmon, Murray mouth:
  mallowe
salt: boodha; bunto; ill-luka;
  tainki
salt bush: bahlaka; naretha;
  yerrear
salt water: ill-luaquasha
sand: karkarook; miyer; munta
sandfly: nanarinyeri
sandhill: alba; tally; wanda
sandpiper: pipipa
sand ridge: urdera
sassafras: caalang
save: daiyuwun; tumbetin
save life: yultun
saviour: tumbutilamaldi
saying: yarnin
scald (verb): klallin
scare (verb): nganden
scatter: kilkilyarin
scold: naiyuwun
scorpion: atnaterta; koongun;
  petachall-lily
scorch: kulkun
scrape: tullun
scratch (verb): wirrannie
screech: tyinkulun

scrub: ita; mallee; ngeragge;
  punthari
sea: lyaleetea; thadelete;
  warringa; warna; woorree;
  woor-oonga
sea, rough: kurrawa
seagull: kirrpiyirrka; munggi-
  wurray-mul; yara
seal: motthari
seashore: thammi
seaweed: bomberry; pinggi;
  wunggi
second: karlowan; wyang
secretly: numald
see: mina; nagooroo; nangana;
  wingaro
see!: nacooma
seed: kulu
seed, edible: kuldoo
seed, grass: doonbur
seed, small black edible:
  munyeru
seek: tuyulawarrin
seize: muranpun; plunden
selfish: thirti
send: konkuwarrin; taiyin
shade: boongala; liliiri; pangari
shade (verb): melkin
shade of trees: carramar
shade tree: kurragong
shadow: minnta; pangari;
  undoolya
shady place: moola
shag: kurrowera
shag, black: yolde
shag, white: puratte
shag, white-breasted: moogana
shake: roralgarin; uc-nun-alemem
shake the head: pilyau-undun
shallow: inberra; thame
shame: inyerra-alcrim;
  oloorinann

share (verb): peranbin; pinpuna
shark: ngrakkani
shark, carpet: wobbegong
shark, tiger: kunara; tealedyan
sharp: padmuri
sharpen: padmurwarrin
she: ba; kitye; yetni
sheep: burra burra; jumbuck
shell: ngipi; niley; wa-ah
shell midden: mirnyong

SHELLFISH:

    arama: bailer shell
    banawara: limpet
    koonwarra: oyster
    kumala: mud shell
    lokure: mussel
    moondara: periwinkle
    munggi: mussel
    namaga: pearl shell
    pundira: conch shell
    tagera: cockle
    tyelokuri: mussel
    wara: oyster
    wela: bailer shell
    wietatenana: nautilus
    yea: mussel
    yerlata: oyster

shelter: mia-mia; nangare; wiltja; wurley
shelter, grass: nunoo
shelter, bark: dardur; gunyah; humpy
shelter, rock or cave: gibber-gunyah
she-oak: kolge; kurtli
shield: alquirta; goolmarry; hillimung; pirramurra; wakkalde; woonda
shield, oval: bamarook
shield, wooden: boreen
shin: cherarra; jorrer
shine: beelarong; klartin
shingleback: garbarli
ship: ngarraraipari; warriuka
shirt: mundarra
shiver: ngionkun
shoal: partyi
shoe: unterlina; turninyeri; urtathurta
shoes, emu: kurdaitcha
shoot (verb): icherramal; popa
shore: dilkera
short: katoa; menurte; tluiye
shortest: tluyeol
shoulder: alliebree; markulde; ungunyer-pollipa
shoulder blade: markulde
shout: kaidundun
show: reyin
shrike, pied crow: tchaceroo; tiltili
shrubs, place of: terrara
shut: muritpun
shut in: muriltpun
sick: halcoppatunein, mendic; minga
sickness: budgel; minga; wiwirri
side: prewirri
sieve (verb): morokkun
sign language: kumaloro
signal, smoke: kowandi
silence: kapo; thoomee
silent: tortuwallin
silver perch: kooberry
silver wattle: currong
sing (verb): beria; boroyah; bundah; poonja; ringbalin; warrannie; wonkana
singe: nyringgen
sink (verb): mirpin

sister: kongaroo; marauwe;
  nowantareena
sister, elder: koongoora;
  maranowe
sister, younger: tarti
sister-in-law: mambo
sit: barribunda; nangalla;
  ningana; nyang; nyinna;
  tergoonee
sit down: allambee; ninnann;
  yangalla
sit on: thopramolla
skin (noun): bungkee; imba;
  pultha; yenpar
skin (verb): wertun
skin, kangaroo: cudgewong
skirt: goomilla
skull: cobbra
sky: goonagulla; illcarrie;
  morang; waiirri; warratinnah
sky, blue: loaranneleah; wullun
sky camp: Bullima
sky, rainy: quasha-ul-kurre
sky, ruler of the: Nepelle
slaty-gum: arangnulla
sleep: bomburra; dora; mia;
  miala; muwe; uncoo;
  ungwyndei; weeronga
sleeping place: woongarra
sleeping place in the bush:
  noonameena
sleepy: muwe watyeri
slow: mant
small: gidju; goobita; katee-
  wailwo; kutyo; minya;
  toogaadya; weema
smell (verb): pendin
smile (verb): kunthamawerana
smoke: boorana; kare; muldi;
  poyyou; pumdo
smoke signal: kowandi
smoke tobacco: muttun; timbelin

smooth: kilkulun
snake: endracoon; koorang;
  upmoa; wobma; wommee

SNAKES: (see also reptiles)

biggarroo: wombat snake
bubbur: large brown and
  yellow snake
daya-minya: small carpet
  snake
goonnear: carpet snake
gununo: black snake
guridjadu: carpet snake
kikinummi: black snake
ngumundi: black snake
nurawordubununa: carpet
  snake
oiyangopan: carpet snake
ooyu-bu-lui: black snake
pranggiwatyeri: tiger snake
taipan: giant brown snake
tintauwa: black snake
tityowe: death adder
uka: white sand snake
waiye: light brown snake
wititurar: small snake
yalakki: carpet snake
yuwam: black snake

snapper: nannygai; wobbegong;
  wollomai
sneeze: injaracna; newchin;
  tyrintyin
snipe: thanpathanpa
snore: normananyee
snow: goonama
so: lun
soak: yalgin
soft: munangpallan; noinpalin
soil: kooruck
soldier-bird: degeen-boya

some: maltaiar
somewhere: winthunga
son: brauwarate; ngauwire
son, eldest: pamgali
song: ringbalin
song, sacred: quabara
sorcerer: boyla; koradji; wirinun; wiwirimalde
sorcery: millin
sore: marma; picca
sorry: ngarpin; parpin
soul: pangari; urrie urrie; yowi
sour: lukun
south: mirreen; nuru-buan; olebyra; rikkara
south-east: bulli-medi-mundi
south-east wind: yarrageh
south-west: gurra
south-west wind: gurra malye
south wind: gooroondoodil-baydilbay; merringannee; nuru-nuru-bin
Southern Cross: Birubi; Chucullba; Koodyoorinadyal; Yaraandoo
sow: wingamin
sow thistle: talga; thalaak
spark: orinjetta; tundi
sparkling: tilpulun
sparrow: neenca
sparrow-hawk: poorparta
speak: kulpana; panelgorana; piyaller; wenkana; yaman; yarnin; yarra
spear: cadgee; gummy; kia; winta; yarnde; yerracharta
spear (verb): pandana; wakkin
spear, acacia wood: gidya
spear, bamboo: pinta
spear, bamboo, with four points: pita
spear, emu: mooroon

spear, fish: gowdalie; punkulde
spear head: borral
spear, jagged: kalkro
spear, large: orumbera
spear, long heavy black: wunde
spear of medicine man: thingairipari
spear, reed: kaike
spear shaft: marrongie
spear tree: etnurra
spear with several barbs: kaiya
spear with stingray barb: wolka
spear with two barbs: pillara
speech: wika
speed: mitamit
spider: brupe; uwoppa; wonka
spider, trapdoor: murga muggai
spill: yaramin
spin: ngembelin
spinifex: iyouta
spirit: mooroop; purkabidni; thambaroo
spirit, bora: gayandi (man's word); gurraymi (woman's word)
spirit, demon: coocoo-loora; marmoo
spirit, dream: Doowi
spirit, drought: Yalkara
spirit, drought (of wirinun): mullee mullee
spirit, evil: brupe; melape; muldarpe; wunda
spirit, familiar: yunbeai
spirit, grand-mother: Puckowe
spirit, great: Baiame
spirit-haunted tree: mingga
spirit land: Bullima
spirits of birth: walla-gudjail-wan; walla-guroon-bu-an
spirits, old: nurrumbunguttia
spit: doleboin; pill-ler

splinter: indenima
split: threllin
spoonbill duck: thowla
sprat, Murray mouth: kungulde
spread: nenartin; wiltun
spring (season): nartee, rewuri
spring of water: brim-brim;
  narmare; prilpulun
spring, spirit of: Yarrageh
spring wind: mayra; yarraga
sprinkle: thrippin
squeeze (verb): moondak; pantin
squirrel, flying: berontha;
  buggoo; butterga; mangaroo;
  pongo; tuan
stab: tolkundun
stake: tappan
stamp: grokumbalin; tolkun
stand: tangulun; yuka;
  yummun
stand up: buckali; tana
star: burley; kulka; pinterry;
  quarallia; tuldar
stare: ngenyarin
stare at: pilkundun; wildin
start (jump with fright): prantin
starve: onengarkwa
stay (verb): yallambee
steady: moranjee; murungar
steal: pettin
steep: perke; rengbari
step (verb): kowundun; ngoppun
stick: holta; kooroorook; wonna;
  yapar
stick, barbed (for catching
  grubs): midjeer
stick, digging: gunni; wanna
stick, fighting: waddy;
  worraworra
stick, man-killing: birra-ga;
  konnung
stick, message: mungi, thriggi

stick, painted (with feathers on
  top): wilgu-wilgu
stick, pointed: dindi
stick, poison: toorli
stick, striking: waddy
stick, talk: tulpi
stick, throwing: bellata; birrana;
  rarramba; taralye; witwit;
  woomera
sticks for beating time:
  tartengk
stiff: paipe
stiffness: milterree
sting (verb): wiitii
stingray: umpara
stink: bucka; pentin; unditter
stir: wuralparin
stomach: bingy; mankuri; weelar
stone: apurta; burnta; eeerilya;
  gibber; marte; mayama; merri
stone for grinding grass seed:
  dayoorl; doori
stone for rain-making: oodoolay
stone knife: muggil
stone, large: burra
stone, magic: gubbera
stone, pounding: wallong
stone tomahawk: karragan;
  kumbu
stony place: mrangalli
stony ridge: morilla
stoop: tingin
stop (verb): balyarta; burra;
  kalyan; nemmin
stop a while: warma
stork: korrorook; monti
storm: kokipijira; willy-willy;
  yarrawah
storm bird: worippa
straight: chucowra; thure
strait: thurar
strange: malde

stranger: merkani; myall;
  yunkara
stream (small tributary):
  mubboon; pani-millie
strength: prityururmi; thalera
strike: balka; mempin;
  poonganyee
string: mintambe; oleara;
  pertorrue; undooeata
**string of wombat or wallaby
  hair:** wariya
stringybark tree: goondool;
  yangoora
strong: matong; piltengi; thilhya
stubborn: intulka; willawallin
stump: ernar; thulye
stump, burnt: wallangar
stupid: arcoona; plombewallin;
  wanbana
Sturt's desert pea: meekyluka
suck: cooan-dunning
suffer: relbulun
sugar: marngowie; pinyatowe
sugar ant: yeramba
sugar bag: maiyatta
sulky: konegerana
summer: booragul; kiata;
  lowalde; welya
summit: barina
sun: allunga; chintoo; deentoo;
  thummyerloo; tonahleah;
  tshinta; uuna; yindi; yhuko
sunbeam: tyelyerar
sun goddess: Yhi
sunlight: nunkalowe
sunrise: baapanannia; wun-u-wa-
  tirring; yhuko pappora
sunset: berringar; wirruna; yhuko
  hippy
sunshine: woornack
superior: oomoomurla
surround: tuldin

suspect: nunde
swallow (bird): menmenengkuri;
  mulundar; waylehmina
swallow (verb): kunkun
swamp: bullook; tainke
swamp duck: tempi
swamp fish: ita; tyeli
swamp oak: billambang
swan: goonawarra; kauerti;
  tumakowaller; youngoloy
swan, black: baiamul; koolyn;
  mooroocoochin
swear: naiyuwun; olumbera
sweat: kanguama; kantarlie
sweat (verb): arcoorie; kangnarra;
  wertuwallin
sweet: bunyarra; kinpin; lerp;
  moruga
sweetness: kumbelin
sweet water: beal
swell: tinkelin
swift: loongana
swift (bird): beerwon
swim: cheropin; pullun; quasha-
  yerra-pichica; thurakami;
  woka
swing: uc-nulla-mull

T

taboo: gunmarl
tadpole: ngikunde
tail: kaldare; kotla; poora;
  whippoo; yanka
take: mummjeeli; plunden;
  pultin; tean
take away: pintamin
take care of: moerpun
take hold: wato
**talisman made of quartz
  crystal:** murramai

talk: tauwa; yabber; yarnimindin
talk stick: tulpi
talk together: jumbunna
tall: albungec-nurra; yulde
tame: nare
tasty: nunkeri; timpin
tattoo: mungaiyuwun; parlcoon
tattoo mark: munggar
tea: nguni; pelberri
teal: barook, ngerake
teal, speckled: koortgang
tear (verb): daraimin; trelin
teat: ippeeculca; papa
tea-tree: kimmuli; nama;
    wirreecoo
tea-tree, broad-leaved: unoyie
teeth: carteta; nerndoa; teeya;
    tuyalie-dusali; undie; yeera
tell: paialla; rammin; tingowun;
    whytalla
thank: kaukau
that: kakie
that here: anaialye
that there: naiyuwe
their: kandauwe
them: kan
then: wanye
there: karthro; munggow;
    nowieya
there: harnakar
they: kar; unengoo
they (two): kenggun
thicket: mallee; yerang
thief: petamalde
thigh: chewenta
thin: kutyeri; yrottulun
think: kungullun
thirst: mungara
thirsty: klallin; moorelli;
    mungara; nantoo
this: hikkai; nia
thistle: tallerk

three: booroora; kabu;
    munkurippa; neppaldar
throat: kalde; kunga-gnarra
throw: wonninny; wunmun;
    youamalla
throw a spear: lakkin
throw away: throkkun
throw down: pinggen
throwing stick: mirla;
    mullamunale; taralye; witwit;
    woomera; yarramba
thumb: maigamaigawa; narkale
thunder: dooloomai; mundara;
    munte; toney
tickle: gidgee; tittimbalin;
    tuckatuck
tide, advancing: moilong
tide, flood: baragoola
tie: premin; pringgarimmin
tiger shark: kunara
timber, large: wyelangta
timber, small: wyelangta
timid: blukkun
tin: poomong
tire: nguldamul-mindin
tired: nguldammulun; pandeanen;
    tarntunnerrin; umbeeramalla
to: angk; ungai
toad: thidnamura
tobacco: cudgel
today: hikkai nungge; karinga;
    yingoorna
toe: pulca; turnar
together: karobran; mullauna;
    yunt
tomahawk: by-a-duk; gweeon;
    karragain; kumbu; taree;
    willara
tomorrow: kanawinkie; minyaka;
    ngrekkald
tongue: kaiaking; tallangge;
    therlinya

TOOLS: see under weapons
tooth: lea; leongatha
top: nglulun
topknot: walla-boondi
topknot pigeon: goola-willeel
torpedo bug: chumbee
tortoise: kinkindele; wangarang; warka; wayembeh
tortuous: gunbower
toss: throkkun
totem: mah; murdu
totem centre: auwa
totem, hereditary: dhe
totem, individual: yunbeai
track: barreng; pukkan; tshina; turnar; yarluke
track (verb): wartin
track (of foot): darri
trapdoor spider: murga muggai
trap, fish: barameda
tread: towun
tree: ernar; wadelang; yape; yuka
tree fern: lapoinya; pooeet
tree, growing: warwanbool
tree, hollow: winani
tree-runner: bibbi
tree, spirit haunted: mingga
tree struck by lightning: binganah
tree, water-holding: goola-gool

TREES:

   angorra: box
   amulla: edible fruit
   arangnulla: slaty-gum
   bael-bael: gum
   balemo: rough-leaved fig
   ballat: native cherry
   ballook: blue-gum
   bangalay: mahogany gum

bangalow: palm
barranduna: brush myrtle
belah: bull-oak
bibbil: broad-leafed box; myrtle
bilkurra: narrow-leaved box
billambang: swamp oak
bimbil: poplar-leaved box
binburra: white beech
bingelima: orange
bira: whitewood
boelgi: willow
boobyalla: acacia; native willow
boodha: rosewood
boomarrah: native plum
booreea: turpentine
boree: weeping myall
bumbel: native orange
bunya-bunya: large tree with edible fruit; pine tree
buriagalah: acacia
burrawang: nut
burrawingie: diamond-leaved laurel
callangun: blue fig
choota: gum
coobah: acacia
coo-in-new: mahogany
coolabah: eucalypt; flooded box
coranderrk: Christmas bush
currong: silver wattle
deenyi: iron-bark
dheal: sacred tree of the Noongaburra tribe
egaie: mangrove
enunta: bean
etnurra: spear
geebung: persoonia
gidya: acacia
goolabah: grey-leaved box

goon-dool: stringybark
gruee: tree with bitter fruit
heeterra: gum
illginga: beefwood
ilumba: Moreton bay ash
irtalie: bean
jarrah (jerrhyl): eucalypt
   species
jinchilla: cypress pine
kakower: fern
kampa: messmate
karri: eucalypt, W.A.
karwin: grass-tree
kimmuli: teatree
kirrang: wattle
kolge: she-oak
konda: cabbage-tree
kowinka: red mangrove
kula: bloodwood
kunakuna: box
kuntyan: pandanus
kurrajong: *Brachychiton*
   populneum
lakkari: honeysuckle; banksia
lapoinya: fern
mao-warang: native pepper
maroo: pine
maroong: pine
midjee: acacia
mowantyi: pine
mubbu: beefwood
mulga: acacia
myimbarr: black wattle
myndee: sycamore
nama: tea-tree
natan: fig
ngarningi: fig
nglaiye: grass-tree
nonga and **noonga:** kurrajong
odenpa: ironbark
orra-curra: desert oak
panpande: cherry

parragilga: narrow-leaved
   ironbark
pimpala: pine
pooeet: fern
pootikkatikka: wattle
pyingerra: pine
quandong: native peach
taree: wild fig
thoopara: native pear
tooart: tuart
toolain: brown wattle
umbellditta: orange
unoyie: broad-leaved tea-tree
wallowa: broom wattle
wandoo: wandoo gum
waratah: flowering tree
warreeah: mountain ash
wilga: dogwood; willow
wirreecoo: tea-tree
wirildar: an acacia
witjuti: acacia
wuri: red gum
wyterrica: wattle
yangoora: stringy-bark
yaraan: white gum
yarrah: river red gum
yarran: an acacia
yerra-coppa: desert oak

trees, clump of: bundara
trees, place of: googoorewon
tremble: ngoinkun
tributary, small: mubboon
trousers: kurrinyerengk
truffle: widdidna
trumpet: didgerido
trumpeter perch: mado
truth: thur
tuber, edible: irriakura
turkey: goomble-gubbon;
   talkinyeri
turn (verb): wandelana

turn inside out: menaikulun
turn over: mackunya;
　ngerakowun
turn round: karlowun
turpentine tree: booreea
turtle: binking; kinkindele;
　turtauwatyeri; wayamba
turtle, sea: miintinta
turtle, swamp: puntyaiya
twenty: boolarra
twilight: pangarinda; wattar
twist: ngempin; yenempun
two: barkool; boola; godarra;
　pullatye
two, only: mundroola

U

umbilical cord: kalduke
umbrella bush: karagata
uncle: kamaroo; kaya; wimmera
uncle (father's side): wanowe
uncle (mother's side): ngoppano
uncooked: erlicha
understanding: kungun
understanding, lack of: wanbana
unfasten: yanedana
unknown: nammuldi
unpleasant: arilperill
untamed: myall
up: karranga; loru; war
upside down: laremuntunt
urine: kumpa; umboa
us: alie; nam
useless: yande; yuntuwarrin

V

vain: plaityingyin
valley: plurampe

vegetable: rata
vein: pillcoo; yarngge
vendetta: dullay-mullay-lunna
Venus: warte
vermin: tittadi
very: murri; pek
vessel, bark (for holding water):
　wirree
vessel, wooden (for holding
　water): bingui; cardeenie;
　coolamon; kanakie; mimbo;
　pitchie; yerra-colya
view, extensive: yurnga
visitor: alkoo
voice: tunggare
vomit: bulkun; holcoppatunein

W

waddy (weapon or club): kanake;
　puri; mooroola
wade: yondun
wail, death: goonai
wait (verb): balyarta; burra;
　ngaralin
wait awhile: ouraka
wakeful: muwityiwallin
wait (verb): koorala; ngopuld;
　tampin; yannathan; yanning
wallaby: mari; pargi; taranna;
　warrew; warta
wallaby, black: bunderra
wallaby, bush: uwurta
wallaby, rock: erawar
wallaby, small: mai-ra
want (verb): mewultun
warm: boorook; molbangen;
　wurtun
warrior: wundurra
wash (verb): gnolo; nyrippin
wasp: undeneya

watch: moerpun
water: apanie; cobbie; gulli; napanopa; nucko; quasha
water bag: gulli-mayah
water-bag, skin: attower
water beetle: boongurr
water, big: warde yallock
water, clear: wyuna
water, deep: binda; parnggi
water devil: Mulloka
water, dirty: ulluricna
water flowing over rocks: goondnomda
water grass: loombrak
water hen: kilkie
water hole: dungel; gilguy; kaga; mandurama
water hole, deep: quashaiperta quorna
water-lily: kaooroo; umpiya
water-lily, blue: arnurna; kanpuka
water-lily, pink: aquaie
water-lily, white: kanpuka
water, little: pirron-yallock
water, muddy: burrumbeet
water rat: biggoon; goomai
water, running: adnamira; burmpa; nunkuluthen
water, salt: ill-luaquasha; yilgi
water, small: quasha-booga
water, spring: narrawa
water, sweet: kiewa
water, sweetened: beal
water, twisting: warriwillah
water vessel: see vessel, water
water, wild: trawalla
waterfall: murrumbooee
watering-place: baringup
waters, meeting of the: wollombi
wattle: kirrang; pootikkatikka; wyterrica

wattle bird: tallarook
wattle, black: myimbarr
wattle, broom: toolain; wallowa
wattle flower: ngolika
wattle, silver: currong; undurra
wave (noun): murdiella; ule
wax cluster berry: chucky-chucky
we: adloo; allena; gnawela; ngodli
we (all of us): yangennanock
we (two): nam; nullegai
weak: pultue

WEAPONS and TOOLS:

alquirta: shield
ammeara: throwing stick
antyan: spear with four points
bamarook: oval shield
barakadan: boomerang
bargan: returning boomerang (not a fighting weapon)
belettah: throwing stick
binyana: chisel
birrana: throwing stick
birra-ga: man-killing stick
boogoo: long club
boondi: club-headed weapon
boreen: wooden shield
bubbera: returning boomerang
bulgoon: stone tomahawk
burgoin: stone tomahawk
by-a-duk: stone tomahawk
dabberi: club
dowak: club
drekurmi: hatchet; knife
gidji: spear
gidya: long spear of acacia wood
goolmarry: shield
gowdalie: hardwood fishing spear

gummy: spear
gweeon: stone tomahawk
hillimung: shield
jerambitty yarka: spear
jimari: stone knife
kaiher: spear
kaike : reed spear
kaiya: stingray barbed spear
kalduke: fighting club
kalkkalk: club
kalti: spear
kama: spear
kana: spear
karkaro: spear
karnick: throwing stick
karragain: stone tomahawk
karu: spear with stone head
keda: boomerang
kertum: boomerang
kia: spear
kiley: boomerang
kondu: club
konnung: man-killing stick
kullack: club
kullin: throwing stick
kunnai: spear
kutha: club
leawill: club with bent head
lianwill: club
likoorler: spear
maki: hunting boomerang
maller: throwing stick
manyeekerrik: spear
marriwirra: club
marpanye: club
mattina: double-pointed club
meralde: quartz-headed spear
metpadinga: club
mirla: throwing stick
miro: throwing stick
mooroola: waddy
mooroon: emu spear

muggil: stone knife
mulla-munale: throwing stick
mulla-murrale: boomerang
naripal: spear
nullanulla: club with heavy head
nunkardeol: short club
nurula pundi: club
orumbera: large spear
panketye: boomerang
pera: club
pilar: spear
pillara: spear with two barbs
pinta: bamboo spear
pirramurra: shield
pita: four-pointed spear
plongg: knobbed weapon for inflicting punishment
punkulde: fish spear
quunder: club
taralye: throwing stick
taree: tomahawk
thingairipari: spear of medicine man
tunta: spear
tura: spear
tuu: three-pointed spear
waaljerrumbuddy kewat: spear
waddy: war club
wadna: boomerang
wakkalde: shield
wangin: boomerang
wantyandyindn: three-pointed spear
wanya: boomerang
warroo: boomerang
watnah: boomerang
wenbener: throwing stick
winta: spear
woggara: wooden battle-axe
wolka: stingray-barbed spear

womah: boomerang
wommurer: throwing stick
woomera: throwing stick
worraworra: fighting stick
wunde: long spear
yandala: spear with one long
point
yarnde: spear
yarramba: throwing stick
yarrum: throwing stick
yarrumba: boomerang
yerracharta: spear
yerrawar: boomerang
youa: throwing stick

wear (verb): ngolun
weather, fine: woorookool
weeping myall: boree; yarran
well (noun): minga; nerntulya;
ulla; wunjugur
west: dinjerra; rumaiy;
weloorarra
west wind: gheeger gheeger;
werderh
wet: tallbee; undunga; wurte;
yalkin
whale: akama; kaandha; kondarle
what: minna; ngongi
what?: yari
when: ungunuk
when?: yaral
where: tang
where?: windarra; whinya
while: pallai
whirlwind: boolee; onbellera;
willy-willy; wurrawilberoo
whistle (verb): obernilimer;
winberongen; winkulun
whistling duck: chipala;
goonaroo; kibulyo; tatea
white: balpi; lill-lill; pitereka
white ant: mirta; odunepa

white cockatoo: garaweh; kaar;
mooy
white man: Amerjig; kupa
white woman: amerjig-orok
whites (ghosts, devils, also
applied to white people):
thambaroo; wunda
whitewood tree: bira
who: ngongi; unnee
whole: ngruwar
whose: nauwe
why: mengye; mind
widow: mambamya; pumo; yakea
widower: randi
wife: berguna; coorie; kurtoo;
murtamoo; yungara
wild (of animals and men):
myall; warrigal
wild: merkani; myall
wild man: myall, purinyeriol
willow, native: boelgi; boobyalla;
wilga
willy wagtail: deereeree;
gumalkoolin; jenning-gherrie;
mugana; tityarokan
wind: barega; boomori;
burramarona; lillkar;
malbooma; may; rawlinna;
wolpa; yarto
wind, contrary: ngrelggimaiyi
wind, hot: kulgarnie
wind, east: gun-ya-mu
wind, north: douran douran
wind, north-west: munde-wudda
wind, south:
gooroondoodilbaydilbay;
nuru-nuru-bin; merringannee
wind, south-east: yarrageh
wind, south-west: gurra malye
wind, west: gheeger gheeger;
wederh
windpipe: kalde; untoo

windy: burando
wing: tyele
wink: kalpulun
winter: kilpanie; kolya; yorte
wiregrass: elilger
wise man: inkata
wish: ellin
withered: meraldi; mirramirildin; pentin; tyiwiwallin
with: al; ungai
woman: gin; kore; loa; lubra; nongo; toora; willawattathuyin; unkee
woman, childless: plotye
woman, married: aragudgeha; hokarra
woman, old: kombona; koon-ja-gilbee; meetawarri
woman, tabooed: goorewon
woman, white: amerjig-orok
woman, young: kamballa; wirreebeeun; yartuwe
woman, young, married: wanty pian
womb: atnar; manyee
wombat: warreen
wombat snake: biggarroo
women, a number of: kumbumbana
women, two: cooroonya
wommera: see throwing stick
wonder: prantin
wonderful: ngranyéri
wood: kurla; mootta; oura; worrue; karrara
wood, dry: erlinya; ernarinjerika

wood duck: goonarook
wood lizard: bu-maya-mul
wool: yingge
word: tunggare
work: wimmin; yakka
worm: miningkar; tyilye
wound (verb): wakkin
wren: lirralirra
wren, emu: puyulle
wrestle: partambelin; yenembelin
wrist: minna; molta; tungge
write: mungaiyin
wrong: wirrangi

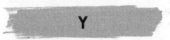

Y

yam: erladger; murr-nong; wotiya; yelka
yam stick: adnumma; gunni
yawn: tappenitin; tarloorin
yearn: duwatyin; parpin mewe
yes: katyill; na-wo; ya-yowi
yesterday: ellow; goolawa; watangrow
you: ngune; neena; nindoah; waimba; yentoo
you (two): lom; ngurle
young: muralappi
young man: kaingani; oolyarra; taldree
young woman: kamballa; wirreebeeun; yartowe
yours: gnoma; nomauwe; ungwynyer

PHRASES AND SENTENCES
ENGLISH–ABORIGINAL

Many Aboriginal languages have been drawn on for the phrases that follow; therefore they must not be considered as coming from a single language, but rather as offering interest and amusement to those who want to add the occasional Aboriginal phrase to their vocabulary.

All right: Cull-la.
Jaba.
Be quick: Iterra.
Bring plenty of money: Mani bumanai nasendag.
Close the door: Muriltp.
Come back: Yaldeenie.
Yawoma.
Come here: Alleari.
Kowia.
Ngai ouri.
Purni ngomerna.
Warrawee.
Come here, boy: Umbacoora.
Come on: Nallak.
Pichi-malla.
Come on, get up!: Hetra akamarei.
Come quickly: Alidgea-guy-pichi.
Come up: Pichi-malla.
Do not have (no got): Arrungwa.
Do not look: Illa winjawtana.
Do not let it go: Illa thorkaninde.
Do not talk so much: Illa Panelgorinba.
Do you hear?: Barrdarrgindo?
Farewell! (said by those who are leaving): Kalyan ungune lewin.

(The reply is: Nginte, or Ngune ngoppun.)
Follow him: War i atyan.
Follow me: War i an.
Get up: Akamarie.
Give me: Gnoka.
Kernaumer.
Unyook.
Give me some water: Koppi unga.
Go!: Ngowalour.
Go away: Brimhillah.
Go away!: Thrunkkun.
Go back: Colba.
Collumbum.
Go on: Albye.
Byeni.
Go to the scrub and bring me some firewood: Punthari ngomerna ngaitshi kurla murrana.
Have you any food?: Hii hii onom takuramb.
He is laughing: Yato kandedana.
He is not there: Nilee.
Hit it: Balka.
How many?: Minyai.
Minyandai.
Munyarai.
Naltra.

How often?: Minyai.
Minyandai.
I am going on a journey:
Jilalan.
Nagugari.
I am sending a message:
Nawargbun djanbin.
I am sulky: Konegrannappa.
I am very hungry: Ngai-i
murnna.
I did not hear: Illa bana noto.
I did not touch it: Illa uatena.
I do not know: Indeato.
I hear: Bana nato.
Barra.
I laugh: Karreda nappa.
I see the dog: Ngai-i yelka mina.
I shall send him: Maduldul
janama.
I sleep: Ngai-i mia.
I speak to you: Kulpernatoma.
I will: El ap.
I will not let it go: Illa
thorkanyerato.
I will not talk so much: Illa
panelgorippa.
Is that your husband?: Kakee
murtanna.
Is that your wife?: Kakee
nongoma.
It is mine: Ninamanima.
It looks like rain: Quasha
illdeegood-munda.
It must be here: Kalyan en el
our.
Let me think: Nangy.
Let us dance: Gar wunalaminju.
Let us eat food: Majin nanarnun.
Listen!: Kungour.
My dear: Gnernpa.
No good: Arcoona.
Quear.

No I'm not: Arrun-derique.
Now I go: Wija narani.
Peace be with you: Yant el our ou.
Put it here: Hik ahk in oura.
Put it there beside you: Yup our
ityan tapangk.
Run!: Iterra.
Speak to me: Kulperaguana.
Stop crying: Thapolo.
Stop talking: Merild our.
Thank you: An ungune. (while
saying this the clasped hands
are thrown away from the
stomach).
There it is: Yate.
The soul will not die: Illa
booker mer ley urrie urrie.
The sun is setting: Allinger
yerra-bamalla.
This place is called. . .: Wuna
wunaia wuniingu. . .
Wait awhile: Ouraka.
Wait for me: Mantanekin.
We are staying there:
Winjidinura.
We are tired: Lal jirgugari.
We did not hear: Illa
banandalie.
We don't understand: Gabo.
We killed the dog: Ngodli yelga
bukana.
We shall come back: Wari
wanjinju.
What do you want?: Nudbur
wungawuduminji.
What is that?: Parepar.
What is the matter?:
Jamanda wule.
Titpeld ellin?
What is your name?:
Wangeganimba.
Yare matye mitye?

What shall I do?: Yarrura.
Where are you going?:
Wungiana?
Which way?: Windana?
Why didn't you wait for me?:
Wana ma nanudagbalaria.
Will you?: Yanima?

You are sulky: Konegranimba.
You bring it back: Yawoma
gumdinda.
You go in front:
Hungararacoola.
You liar: Orra-jerra.
You walk: Yentoo yanning.

THE LORD'S PRAYER

in the Darling River language, which was in use for
500 miles along its length:

Ninnana combea, innara inguna Karkania,
Munielie nakey, Emano pumum culpreathiea,
ona Kara canjelka yonagh patua, angella,
Nokinda ninnana kilpoo yanice, Thickundoo
Wantindo ninnana Illa ninnana puniner,
thullaga, Thilltill Chow norrie morrie
munda, lullara munie.   Euelpie.

The superior figures shown in the following list refer to the following geographical areas:

1. Western Australia
2. South Australia
3. Northern Territory
4. Victoria
5. New South Wales
6. Queensland
7. Tasmania
8. Central Australia

WORD LIST
ABORIGINAL–ENGLISH

A

aalbawal[3]: head
abbulduppi[3]: cold
adaka-palai: let out
adjemot[4]: bad
adjo[1]: I
adjunepa[8]: goanna
adloo[2]: we
adnamira[8]: flowing, running water
adnummer[8]: yam stick
aiain: see aya
aijal[3]: sky
ainbu[3]: rain
aitye barkolo[6]: three
aka[6]: ground
akama[6]: whale
akamarei[8]: get up
al[2] (ald): with
alaijah: see kalajah
alait[3]: dog
alajah: see kalajah
alaok[3]: child
alba[8]: sandhill
albungec-nurra[8]: tall
albye[8]: go on
Alchera: place where the 'Old
   People' lived
Alcheringa: Dreamland, or the
   Land of Baiame
algooma[8]: eating
alguna[2]: drink (verb)
alie: us
alinjarra[8]: north

aljerer[8]: dream
alkingar[8]: eye
alknarar-killja[8]: blind
alknarlba[8]: hip
alkoo: visitor
alkoomie: good
allabuckinee[8]: rain
allambee[4]: sit down, recline,
   remain (verb)
allambie: quiet place
allang-goola[8]: nostril
allar[8]: nose
alleari[8]: come here
alleena: we
alli[3]: dog; moon
alliebree[8]: shoulder
allinger: see allunga
allirra[8]: quartz
allue[8]: liver
allunga (allinger, arlunya): sun
allydung[3]: hear
almeju[3]: fish
alondji[3]: sky
aloota[8]: kangaroo rat
aloripma[8]: flame
alpugi[3] (elpugi): kangaroo
alquirta[8]: shield
alta[8]: hair
alteripa[8]: claypan
alye[2] (alyalle): here
alyenik[2]: near me
amayworra[8]: Orion's Belt
ambe[2]: for
ambo[8]: egg
amerjig: white man

amerjig-orok: white woman
ammaboolah[3]: fish
ammeara[8]: throwing stick
ammijeeler[3]: blood
ammonga[8]: see mongana
ammoula[8]: nose
ampan[6]: cut
amulla[6]: tree with edible fruit
an[2]: me
anaialye[2]: that there
anangkwarrin[2]: prepare
an anyril[2]: for them
anauwe: see nganauwe
anbirik[3]: hill
andek[2]: away (from the speaker)
andi[5]: who
andowach:[6] see
andri[2]: mother
angaikbirig[3] (arnarigbirij): mouth
angbal[3]: hair
angk[2]: into, to
angorra[8]: box tree
angorra: see engorra
anjee-malla[8]: climb
anjigi[3]: hand; teeth
anka[6]: barramundi
ankana[2]: make
anowah[6]: give
antyan[6]: spear with four prongs
antye[8]: give
anyir[2]: from
apa: see appa
apanie: water
apari[2] (apirrie): father
apmurika[8]: boy
appa[6] (apa): water
appointa[8]: cold
appunga[8]: cane grass
apurta[8]: stone
aquiaie: pink water-lily
aragoodgeawonga[8]: adolescent girl
aragudgeha[8]: married woman

arama[6]: bailer shell
arami[2] (urumi): for
aramut[3]: star
arangnulla: slaty gum
arcoona[8]: no good, stupid
arcoorie[8]: sweat
arcurrata[8]: plain
argadba[3]: star
argoonie[8]: catch (verb)
arika: blue water-lily
arilperill[8]: unpleasant
arinya: kangaroo
arkoola: hair
arlunya: see allunga
armoolya[8]: jew lizard
arnarigbirij: see angaikbirig
arndu[2]: come
arntuney[8]: lick (verb)
arnurna: blue water-lily
aroitj[3]: child
aroitja[3]: small
aroo: fan of emu tail feathers
aroo[4]: cygnet
arracoola[8]: front
arrah-cardie[8]: daylight
arrainya[8]: name
arrakata (aruckata): mouth
arrakutcha: snake woman
arrama[8]: louse
arrie-enpa[8]: lip
arrilla: aborigine
arrinyenin[8]: circle
arruleta[8]: neck
arrungwa[8]: do not have (no got)
arrunja[8]: devil
arrurrer[8]: kangaroo
artippa[8]: back
artoo[2]: I
aruaramba[3]: mouth
aruaroli[3]: foot
aruckata: see arrakata
arunta: white cockatoo

arutchie: native ferret, cat or tiger cat
atchina[8]**:** mine
atna[8]**:** womb
atnalure[8]**:** blood
atnaterta[8]**:** scorpion
atninebeemalla[8]**:** kick
atnitta[8]**:** belly
atta[6]**:** I
attong-giuilina[8]**:** cough
attower: skin water bag
atwa[8]**:** man
atye: see kitye
atyimba[6]**:** emu
au[2]**:** now
auminthina: remain (verb)
auwa[6]**:** hole, totem centre
awadabir[6] (rawadabir): goanna
awring-gamalla[8]**:** daylight
aya[3] (aiain, kaain): stone

B

ba[2]**:** he, it, she
baal[5] (bael, bail, bal): expression of disapproval; don't, no, not
baan[4]**:** dog
baanya[5] (baanga): camp
baapanannia: sunrise
baarlijan: platypus
babaneek: mother
babuk[4]**:** mother
bael: see baal
baelbael: gum tree
bagan[4]**:** sit
bagan[6]**:** sea
bagrook[4]**:** woman
bahal[5]**:** tree
bahlaka: salt bush
Bahloo[5]**:** moon, god of the moon, guardian of girls and women

bahn[5]**:** mistletoe
Baiame[5] (Byamee): culture hero or god, creator; literally, Great One
baiamul[5] (byahmul): black swan
baibaiye[2]**:** leaf
bail: see baal
bailaquar (bailiqua): bullock
bailpuli: see bilpuli
bailpulun[2]**:** foolish; forget
bakkano[2]**:** grandmother (maternal)
bakkare[2]**:** grandchild (maternal)
bal: see baal
bal[1]**:** he, it, she
balemo: rough-leaved fig tree
balgon: see bulgoon
balgoungo: chop (verb)
balgul bullalel[1]**:** they
balgun[1]**:** they
balka[5]**:** hit, strike
ballamballam: see bullabulla
ballarat: camping place
ballat: cherry tree
balleroo: rain god
ballook: blue gum tree
balpewallin[2]**:** clean
balpi[2]**:** white
balumbah[3]**:** rain
balun: river
baluni[5]**:** die
balyarta[5]**:** stop, wait
bamarook (bamerook): oval shield
bambra: mushroom
bamburr: kangaroo
bamerook: see bamarook
bami[2]**:** girl
bananee[6]**:** dew
banarra: ear
banawara: limpet
bandera[6]**:** reed
band ngatoa[5]**:** I
bang[4]**:** hut

bangalay[5]: timber of the eucalypt

bangalow[5, 6]: feathery-leaved palm with edible leaves

bangnalla: golden perch

banjeeri: voice of ancestor spirit

banjora: native bear

banool: hill

banya: black-tailed possum

bara[5]: they

baragoola: flood tide

barakadan[6]: boomerang

baralgar: see brolga

barameda: fish trap made of logs

barega: wind

bareki: water

bargan[5] (barragan): returning boomerang

bargi[5] (bargie): grandmother (maternal)

barina: summit

baringa: light

baringup[1]: watering place

barkalonuke[5]: three

barkolobarkolo[5]: four

barkool (barkolo[5, 6]): two

barloona[2]: die

barn[4]: small

barno[2]: aunt

barook: teal

barperipna: morning

barragan: see bargan

barramundi: giant perch

barranduna: brush myrtle

baree: mountain

barreng: track

barribinda: sit (verb)

barrow: see parru

barru[1]: blood

barru[2]: meat

bartill[8]: parrot

bartoo[8]: man

bartoo-gilbee[8]: old man

bartungaran[8]: drop

bato kokoin[5]: water

battana[6]: hit

battur[6]: great

batturi[2]: bundle, heap

baylingyan[3]: die

baynilla[3]: girl

beal[4, 5] (bool, bull): water sweetened with honey from the flowers of a Banksia

beal: see belah

beanga[5]: father

bedgery: see pitchery

beeargah: see biaga

beebeethung: red

beekbeek: ear

beela[5] (beeleer, beeler): black cockatoo

beela: see belah

beelang: bag

beelarong: shining

beeleer: see beela

beenak (binnap): basket

beenarra[3]: ear

beer[5]: long distance

beeree: lagoon

beereegan: quail

beereek: native cat

beereeun: small prickly lizard

beerwon: swift (bird)

beewee: goanna

beeyung: father

began[6]: beat

belah (beal, beela, belar, billah): bull oak tree

belettah[3] (bellata): throwing stick

bemkeah[5]: man whose brother is dead

benalla: musk duck

benang[4]: husband

benedba[3]: he, it, she

bengero[4]: two
bengeroganme[4]: three
bengeroobengeroo[4]: four
benjiman: husband
berallah: musk duck
berguna (biergoonera): wife
beri: claw
beria: sing
berigora[5]: orange-speckled duck
berley[5]: bait
berlkie[5]: see burlkie
bernarro[4]: gum tree
berontha: crow
berrimilla[5]: kingfisher
berringar[6]: sunset
Ber-rook-boorn: the first man
bertana[6]: day
Berwooland Babinger: god, son
of Pundjel
betcheri: see budgeree
betcherrygah: budgerigar
bettulun[2] (brattulun): disturbing
from sleep
bi[1]: fish
biaga[5] (beeargah): hawk
biangri: night
biara: moon
bibba[6]: hill
bibbi[5] (bibbee): tree-runner
bibbil[5]: broad-leaved box tree;
eucalypt
biergoonera[6]: see berguna
biggarroo: wombat snake
bigge[6]: sun
biggoon[5]: water rat
bigha[2]: moon
bilba[5] (bilber, bilbie, bilby):
bandicoot, bandicoot rat
bilbungra: pelican
bilcom[5]: setting fire to a wurley
bilkurra: narrow-leaved box tree
billa[1,5,6] (bilo, pilly): river; water;

fish. The common word billy,
the tin can for holding and
boiling water, came originally
from billa
billabong[5,6]: pool separated from a
river
billah: see belah
billai[5] (billay): crimson-winged
parrot
billambang: swamp oak
billeang: bat
billoo[5]: men with eagles' feet
billungah: creek
billy: see billa
bilo[1]: river (see also billa)
bilpuli[2] (bailpuli): fat, marrow
bilyana (bilyara[5]): wedge-tailed
eagle
bilyarra[4]: eagle
bimbil: poplar-leaved box wood
tree
bimble: earth
bimbinya[5]: jealousy
binburra: white beech tree
binda: deep water
bindar[5]: kangaroo
bindaree: river
bindi[6]: see bingy
bindha[5] (bindeah): prickle
bing[6]: father
bingami: mopoke
binganah: tree struck by lightning
bingarra: bark
bingelima: native orange tree
binga-wingul[5] (bingahwingul):
needle bush
bingee: see bingy
bingge-la[5] (bingehlah): exclamation
or ejaculation meaning, 'You
can have it!'
binghi: brother, later applied to all
aborigines

bingui[5] (binguie): wooden vessel, shaped like a canoe, for holding water

bingy[5] (bindi, bingee, binji): belly, stomach

binking[4]: turtle

binnap: see beenak

binyana[5] (binyanner[3]): chisel

biram[6]: heavens, sky

birra-ga[5]: stick for killing a man

Birrahgnooloo: see Birra-nulu

birra-li[5] (birrahlee, birrah-li): baby, girl

birrana: throwing stick

Birra-nulu[5] (Birrahgnooloo): Baiame's first wife. The name means 'face like a tomahawk handle'

birrarl[5]: an exclamation

birrawa: go down

birri[5]: boy

birree gougou: see birri gu gu

birrie: danger

birri gu gu[5] (birree gougou): a call to encourage someone to attack

Birubi[6]: Southern Cross

birwain[6]: bulrush

birwain[6]: boy

biteyee[3]: good

bittoorong[5]: red

blukkun[2]: afraid, alarmed, timid

blungbai[5]: father

boang[6]: die

bobbin[6]: father; moon

bodalla[5]: place where a child is tossed in the air

boelgi: willow

boge (bogey, bogie): bathe

bogong: see bugong

bohra[5] (bohrah, bowrah): kangaroo

bokara[5]: heat

bokka[4]: dog

boko[4]: head

boko: blind

boloke: lake

bolool: night

bombery: seaweed

bomboora: reef of rocks usually found at the foot of a cliff

bomburra: sleep

bonanyong: see buninyong

bonelya[5]: bat

bong[6] (bung): boy

bonganah[4]: boy

bonja[5]: hut

boobialla: see boobyalla

boobook: mopoke

booboo-tella[5]: feather from an emu's tail

boobyalla (boobialla): acacia, native willow

boodgeri: see budgeree

boodha[5] (budta, budtah, budtha): rosewood tree; salt

boodjerrie: see budgeree

boogarah[4]: keep away

boogoo[5]: long club

boogoo-doo-ga-da[5] (boogoo-doogahdah): rain bird

bookabooda: native gooseberry

bookang[4]: night

bookooi: rain

bool: see beal

boola (boolaboo, boolara, bolloween, bulli): two

boolaroo[6]: two

boolarra: twenty

boolea: cold

boolee[5]: whirlwind

boolgana: kangaroo

booloman[4]: two

booloman batha kootook[4]: three

booloman bathra boolung[4]: four

boolongena: emu
boolool: dark
boolooral: see bulooral
booloot[4]**:** above, heavens, sky
boolpooli[2]**:** chalk
booltaroo: canoe
boolungal: pelican
Boomajarril: place of flowers where fairies congregate
Booma-ooma-nowi[5] (Boomahoomahnowee): the son of Baiame
boomarrah: native plum tree
boomayamayamul and **boomayahmayahmul:** see bumaya-mul
boomerang: weapon for throwing. The word is of doubtful origin. It is said that there is a close connection between the words for wind (boomori) and boomerang in some districts. Early forms of the word were boomering and bummering
boomori: wind
boonamin: sand hill god
boonari: 'big boss'; anything supernatural
boondar: kangaroo
boonderoo: stony country
boondi[5] (boondee): club-headed weapon
boondoon: kingfisher
booner: beach
boongala: shade
boongurr: water beetle
boor[4]**:** one
boora and **boorah:** see bora
boorabi: see boor-bee
booral[5]**:** big, high
boorala: good
booragul: summer

booran: pelican
boorayo[4]**:** day
boor-bee: native bear
boorana: smoke
booreah[6]**:** fire
booreea: turpentine tree
boorlee[2]**:** see burley
boorook: warm
booroora (dooroogai): three
booroowal: day
boorrang: mist
bootoolga[5] (bootoolgah): blue-grey crane
booyanga (boyanga): egg
booyangan: female
bopup[4]**:** boy
bor (bur): girdle of manhood; circle
bora[5] (boora, boorah, borah): initiation ceremony. The word probably comes from bor, the girdle of manhood, worn in initiation ceremonies
borak[5]**:** banter, fun
boree: myall, weeping myall
boreen[5]**:** wooden shield
boringkoot: native raspberry
boroya: sing
borral[1]**:** spear head
borrinyer[5]**:** live (verb)
borun[4]**:** night
bougong: see bogong
bowrah: see bohra
boyanga: see booyanga
boyla: sorcerer
brael[4]**:** star
bra kini[4]**:** man
bralgah: see brolga
brate: see brauwarate
brattulun[2]**:** see bettulun
brauwarate[2] (brate): son, younger son

brenbun[4]: wife

bret[4]: hand

bri: see buri

brigge: messenger

brimbrim[4]: spring of water

brimhillah: go away

brinawa: place where water lilies grow

brolga[5] (baralga, bralgah): native companion

broon[4]: day

brumby: wild horse. It is doubtful whether it is an aboriginal word

brupe[2]: devil, evil spirit; spider

bruye[2]: forehead

buba[5]: father

buba-larmay[5] (bubahlarmay): game in which the players jump into the water with a splash

bubbera[5] (bubberah): boomerang that returns

bubbur[5] (bubburr): large brown and yellow snake

bucka[5] (puka): stink

buckali[8]: stand up

buckandee and **buckandeer**: see bukkandi

buckna[4]: rain

buddang[6]: mother

buddawong: see burrawang

budgel: sickness

budgeree[5] (boodgeri, budgeri): excellent, good

budgerigar: small bird also known by several aboriginal names, and by early settlers as warbling grass parrakeet, shell parrot, zebra grass parrakeet, etc.

budjor[1]: land

budta, budtah, and **budtha**: see boodha

buggoo[5]: flying squirrel

bugong (bogong, bougong): grey moth

bukkandi[5] (buckandee, buckandeer): native cat

bukkum[6]: land

bular[5] (bullae): two

bularbular[5]: four

bulga-nunnoo[5] (bulgahnunnoo): insects (literally bark-backed i.e. under bark and logs)

bulgoon[6] (balgon): stone tomahawk

bulkun[2] (bulgen): vomit

bull: see beal

bulla bulla[5] (ballam ballam, bullah bullah): butterfly

bullae[6]: see bular

bullai bullai[5]: green parrot

bullarrto: place of plenty

bullen bullen: lonely place

bulli[2]: see bodla

Bullima[5] (Bullimah): Spirit Land, heaven, Sky Camp

bulli-medi-mundi[5] (bullimedeemundi): south-east

bullito[4]: big

bulln bulln[5]: lyre bird

bullook: swamp

bullula[4]: kangaroo

bullyee[8]: navel

buln buln: green parrot

bulooral[5] (boolooral:) night owl

bulpuli[2]: lime; pipeclay

bu-maya-mul[5] (boomayamayamul, boomayahmayahmul): wood lizard, responsible for creating human babies

bumbel[5] (bumble): native orange tree

bunan[6]: make

bundah[6]: sing

bundara: clump of trees; edge of
  swamp
bunderra: black wallaby
bung: see bong
bungun bungun: see bun-yun
  bun-yun
buninyong (bonanyong): man
  lying on back
bungkee[8]: skin
bunmil[4]: hill
bunmilla[5] (bunmillah): fish
bunna[5]: cannibal
bunnener[5]: make
bunnyal: see bun-yal
bunnyyarl: see bun-yal
bunora[5]: long distance
bunto[8]: salt
buntor[8]: big
bunya-bunya: large tree with
  edible fruit, pine tree
bun-yal[5] (bunnyal, bunnyyarl): flies
bunyarra: sweet
bunyip: legendary monster, usually
  supposed to live in lakes. An
  early account of a native
  tradition describes it as 'bigger
  than an elephant, like a bullock,
  with eyes like live coals, and
  with tusks like a walrus's'
bun-yun bun-yun[5] (bungun
  bungun): frog
bupper[6]: three
bur: see bor
burando[6]: windy
burgoin[5]: stone tomahawk
buri[5] (bri): acacia
buriagalah: species of acacia,
  literally place of the buria tree,
  sometimes corrupted to
  brigalow
burley[5] (boorlee, burle): star
burlkie[5] (berlkie): hair

burmpa: running water
burndo[5]: fish
burnta[2] (parnta): stone
burnu[1]: tree
burra: stop (verb), wait (verb);
  light (adj); large stone
burrabee: blood
burraburra: busy; quick; sheep
burrakay[3]: hill
burramaronga: wind
burramundi[6] (barramunda):
  Burnett salmon
burrandool: quail
burrawang (burwan): nut tree
burrawingie: diamond-leaved
  laurel
burremah: bring, come
burrendong: native bear
burrengeen: peewit
burrumbeet: muddy water
burudburang[3]: big
burwan: see burrawang
butterga[5] (buttergah): species of
  flying squirrel
buumbuul: manna
buyi[1]: stone
by-a-duk: stone tomahawk
byahmul: see baiamul
Byamee: see Baiame
byenie[8]: go on

C

caalang: sassafras
caberra: see cobbra
cabon: great, large
cadgee[8]: spear
caehngao[6]: snake
calca[4]: star
calimpa: bees' nest
callangun: blue fig

callemondah: many hills
caloola[5]**:** climb (verb)
canajong[7]**:** Tasmanian plant with edible fruit and leaves, known as pigface
cangella[6]**:** good
cappy[4]**:** water
carawatha: place of pine trees
carbethon: glad
carbora: native bear; water worm
cardeenie[8]**:** water vessel
cardo[4]**:** man
carina: bride, girl-wife
carlik[4]**:** four
carloo[8] **:** penis
carltooka[8]**:** bulldog ant
carndarah[6]**:** see kandara
carnka[8]**:** crow
carpoo[4]**:** three
carramar[6]**:** shade of trees
carrangall: athletic
carroo[8]**:** creek
carteta[8]**:** teeth
cartoo[8]**:** father
challing[4]**:** tongue
chenka: finish
cherrara[8]**:** shin
cheropin[8]**:** swim
chewenta[8]**:** thigh
chicha[4]**:** small
chillberto[8]**:** rain
chilla[8]**:** poison fish
chillkalla[8]**:** prickle
chinkayackaby[4]**:** day
chinna[4, 8]**:** foot
chintillga[8]**:** grasshopper
chintoo[8] (chinto)**:** sun
chintu-ruigin: daylight
chipala: whistling duck
chippia[8]**:** duck
chooka-chooka[8]**:** dream
chookola[8]**:** hole

choota[8]**:** gum tree
chucky-chucky: wax cluster (an edible berry)
chucowra[8]**:** straight
Chucullba[8]**:** Southern Cross
chumbee: torpedo bug
churinga: bullroarer (see also tjurunga)
cobbie[8] (kabee, koppie)**:** water
cobbra[5, 6, 7] (caberra, kabbera, kabura, kappara, kobbera, kobra, kobul)**:** head, skull
cobbycoononyee[8]**:** rain (verb)
cobbyworrall[8]**:** rain (verb)
cocararra[8]**:** east
cockalella[8]**:** white cockatoo
cockanoorah[4]**:** hair
cocker[4] (cocki)**:** head
colac and **colah:** see koala
colba[8]**:** go back
coleenie[8]**:** hear
collenbitchick: species of ant; double star in Capricornis
collin[4]**:** fire
collumbum: go back
colo: see koala
color[8] (warruc-color)**:** flame
combo[1, 3, 6]**:** white man who lives with an aboriginal woman
comebee: see kumbi
comebo and **comeboo:** see kumbu
comebunyee[8]**:** hot
cooan-dunning[8]**:** suck
cooba: black stingless bee
coobah (koobah)**:** special of acacia
coocoo-loora[8]**:** demon spirit
coo-ee (cooey)**:** the call the aborigines gave to summon anyone, and quickly adopted by white settlers. One early explanation of the meaning was 'Come to me'

coo-in-new: mahogany tree
coola: angry
coola: see koala
coolabah[5]: eucalypt, flooded box tree
coolabun: native bear
coolah: tree
coolamon[6] (coolaman, kooliman): wooden vessel for holding water or seeds, often made from a hollowed knot of a tree. Sometimes used as a term for the knot
coolbaroo: old
coolbyngga[8]: drawing, painting
cooler[5]: angry
coolie: sun
coolley[4]: tree
cooloongatta: fine view
cooma (combah, gaoma, kuma): one
Coon undhurra: dragonfly woman
coondanie[8] (coontannie): cut (verb)
coonmidjender[3]: sea
coorabin: barking lizard
cooragook: pause, wait
coorah[4]: woman
coorang: brown gravel
coordaitcha: see kurdaitcha
coorie[5]: husband, wife, spouse
coorigil[5] (corrigel, courigul): sign of bees
cooroo[8]: eye
cooroonya: two women
cootrah[4]: two
cope cope: large lake fed by water from smaller lakes
coradgee: see koradji
coranderrk[4]: Victorian Christmas bush; wilga
cornu tribe[6]: hair
corowa[7]: rocky river

corrigel: see coorigil
corroboree[5] (corobboree and similar spellings): dance; meeting
courigul: see corrigel
cowirrie: rat
cudgel: tobacco
cudgewong: kangaroo skin
cue-on-buntor[8]: girl
cue-on-mema[8]: little girl
culgoa: river running through
cullebee[8]: hip
cullgenborn[8]: cough
cull-la(cull-lar): all right
culma: spiny fish
cumbee: see kumbi
cundoonie[8]: kick (verb)
Cunmurra: carpet snake god
cunnenbeille and **cunnunbeille:** see kunnan-beili
curbarra: plenty
curla[6]: fire
currajong: see kurrajong
currawang: bell or black magpie, donkey bird, crow shrike
curreiquinquin: butcher bird
curringa: black duck
currong: silver wattle
curta[8]: head

D

dabber[6]: club
daen[5]: aborigine
daiyuwun[2]: keep, save
daku[2]: sand
dala[3]: eyes
dalo[6]: fire
dalthing[5]: end, finish
dalyo[5]: light (adj)
dandaloo[5]: beautiful

daraimin[5]: tear (verb)

dardur[5] (dardurr): shelter made of bark

darinana[5]: to put a water vessel near a fire

darri: track (of foot)

daya-minya[5] (dayah-minyah): small carpet snake

dayoorl[5]: flat stone used for grinding grass seed

dealk[4]: good

deentoo[2]: sun

deenyi[5]: ironbark tree

deereeree[5]: willy wagtail

degeen-boya[5] (degeen-boyah): soldier bird

dertoo[2]: hill

dhe[1, 5]: hereditary totem

dheal[5]: sacred tree

dheran[6]: gully

dhilla: hair

diale[5]: food

didjeridoo (didjerido[3]): musical instrument, trumpet

dilkera: edge, shore

dilli[5, 6] (dillee, dilly): bag for holding possessions, usually made of grass, cord, or fur. Although dilli means bag, the usual term is dillybag. Dilli was originally fine wood dust, and the dilli bag was used to carry sticks and tinder for fire-making, and the term extended to other bags

dindi[5] (dindee): pointed stick

dindin[4]: bad

dinewan[5]: emu

dinga[4]: stone

dinjerra[5] (dinjerrah): west

dirdi[6]: day

dirrang: another term for dilli, q.v.

ditji toda[2]: day

ditter (ditta): mud, soft ground

ditye[2]: sun

dityiwakka[2]: star

djaat[1]: sun

djiimang[1]: see

djui[1]: bad

doleboin[8]: spit

dombart[1]: one

dombock: see jombock

dooliba[5] (dulibah): bald

dooloomai[5]: thunder

doonbur[5] (doonburr): grass seed

doongara[5] (doongairah): lightning

doonkami: rise (verb)

doonkuna: rising

dooran dooran[5]: see douran douran

dooroogai: three

doori[5]: grindstone

Doowi[5] (Doowee, Dowee): dream spirit

dora[4]: sleep

douran douran (dooran dooran, dourandowran): north wind

dowak[1] (dowak wirba): club

drekin[2]: chip (verb)

drekurmi[2]: hatchet, knife

drikdrik[4]: limestone

droonoodoo (droonooda): dream circle

dta[1]: mouth

dtallang[1]: tongue

dulibah: see dooliba

dullay-mullay-lunna[5] (dullaymullaylunnah): feud (literally vengeful hatred)

dulloora[5] (dulloorah): small grey bird

dumbog: see jombock

dumer[5] (dumerh, dummerh): brown pigeon

dummal[6]: small
dummerh: see dumer
dunburra-gee[3]: teeth
dundaldyn[6]: woman
dungel[5] (dungle): water hole
dunnum[6]: tongue
durabunun[6]: hut
durda[1] (durdd): fish
durdaak: pipeclay
durellie[5]: fight (verb)
durnin[6]: hand
durri[5] (durrie): cake made of flour
  ground from grass seed
durroon[5]: night heron
duwatyin[2]: yearning
dyintan[6]: nail fish

E

eake[3]: water
earmoonan and **ear-mounan**: see
  eer-moonan
echuca: meeting of the waters
echunga[2]: short distance
ecmurra[8]: big
edpeddo[3]: child
eebi: ghosts which inhabit the
  bodies of men
eehu[5]: rain
eeo eeo: alas!
eer-dher[5] (eer-dheer): mirage
eerilya: stone
eerin[5]: small grey owl
eer-moonan[5] (earmoonan, ear-
  mounan): monster (literally long
  sharp teeth)
egaie: mangrove
eggwarna[8]: see engwarnar
el[2]: is
elanora: home by the sea
el ap: I will

eleanba wunda[5] (eleanbah
  wundah): spirit monsters with
  two toes which live in the
  underworld
elilger: wire grass
elleenanaleah: beauty
ellhimalla[8]: day
ellimatta: our home
ellimeek: my home
ellin[2]: see ennin
ellin: move
elloi-jerra (eloi-jerra): large lizard
ellow[5]: yesterday
ellulger: ice
elod[3]: foot
eloin[3]: man
eloitj[3]: small
elouera: pleasant place
elpugi[3]: see alpugi
elunba: armpit
enamalla[8]: catch (verb)
enborra: heavy
enca[4]: one
endota[8]: beautiful
endracoon[8]: snake
engoordna: boil (noun)
engorra (angorra): bank
engwarnar (eggwarna): bone
engwura: initiation ceremony
enmaraleek[4]: give
enna[3]: nose
ennin[2] (ellin): have, wish
entoo[8]: feather
enunta[8]: bean tree
era cunalerme: play (verb)
erad[3]: one
erawar[8]: rock wallaby
erladgeer[8]: yam
erlicha[8]: raw, uncooked
erlinya: dry wood
ernar[8]: tree; stump of tree
ernar-injerika[8]: dry wood

errabunga: fish
erricha: arm
erringer[8]**:** neck
erringerrcoogum[3]**:** heat
err-reedy[8]**:** long time
errurraga: dry
ertargwar[8]**:** rat
etninja[8]**:** moon
etnurra: spear tree
etrakee[8]**:** lazy
euahl: see wahl
euloomarah: see yulu-mara
euloowirree: see yulu-wirree
eumina: repose
eurabbie: blue gum
eurah[5]**:** drooping shrub
eurobin: lagoon at foot of
    mountain

G

gaarn[4]**:** nose
gaat[4]**:** mouth
gabo: we don't know
gahrahgah: see ga-ra-ga
galah[5] (gilah): pink-breasted parrot
    or rose-breasted cockatoo
gallang[6]**:** good
gamboden[4]**:** one
Ganba: large mythical snake
gandjari[6]**:** bony bream
gaoma[2]**:** see cooma
ga-ra-ga[5] (gahrahgah, garargah):
    crane
garalin[2]**:** delay
garaweh[5]**:** white cockatoo
garbai[5]**:** forehead band made of
    string
garbarli[5] (garbarlee): shingleback
garganj[6]**:** chicken hawk
gauware[2]**:** deep

gauwel[2]**:** midday
gaya-dari[5] (gayardaree): platypus
gayandi[5] (gayanday, gayandy):
    bullroarer, and therefore also a
    man's name for a bora spirit or
    bora devil. The woman was not
    allowed to use this name, but
    said gurraymi
gayardaree: see gaya-dari
gedala[1]**:** day
geebung[6] (geebong): Persoonia tree
    and also its fruit
geenong: footprint
geera[4]**:** see ghera
geewan: common fern
geewinnia[8]**:** see uwinnia
gelane[2]**:** elder brother
gelar[2]**:** brother
gena[4] (gerra): blood
geppmorra (gepmorra): fingernail
gerai[6]**:** sand
gerra[2]**:** see gena
gerringong: afraid; ambush
gheeger gheeger[5]**:** west wind
ghera (geera): gum leaf
ghilgai: see gilguy
Ghinda-inda-mui[5] (Ghinda-
    hindahmoee): son of Baiame
gibber: rock, stone
gibber-gunyah: cave dwelling
    (gibber: rock; gunyah: shelter)
giddea: see gidya
giddie[8]**:** resin
gidgee (gidgeena): tickle
gidgee: see gidya
gidgerigar[5] (gidgereegar,
    gidgeereegah): small parrot
    (budgerigar), warbling grass
    parrot
gidji[1]**:** spear
gidju[6]**:** small
gidya[5, 6] (giddea, gidgee): acacia

tree; long spear made of this timber

gilah: see galah

gilanggur[6]**:** good

gilguy[5] (ghilgai, ghilghi): water hole

gimbi[5]**:** make

gin: aboriginal woman. Very occasionally used for female kangaroo

gira[6]**:** tree

girraween[5] (girrahween): place of flowers

giwar[5]**:** man

gnahwo: see na-wo

gnally geletcho[4]**:** we

gnamma: hole; rock

gnawela[5]**:** we

gnernpa[5]**:** my dear

gnertown[5]**:** a number of people

gnoka[5]**:** give, give me

gnolo[5]**:** wash; two people

gnoma[5]**:** yours

gnooloo-gail: see nulu-gail

gnoolooyoundoo: see nulu-yoon-du

gnopowa[5]**:** two people

gnoyalanna[5]**:** afraid

goannar[6]**:** hut

goberta[8]**:** plum bush

goborro: dwarf box

goburra: see kookaburra

godarra[8] (kutthara): two

goditcha: see kurdaitcha

gogobera: see kookaburra

gondol[6]**:** canoe

goobita[8]**:** small

gooboothoo: done

goochagoora[8]**:** one

goodoo[5]**:** codfish

googarh[5]**:** goanna

googoorewon[5]**:** place of trees

goo-goor-gaga[5] (goug gour gahgah, gougourgahgah, gourgourgahgah): laughing jackass (literally take a stick)

go-oh[5]**:** come

goohnai: see goonai

goolabah: grey-leaved box tree

goola-gool[5] (goolahgool, goolahyool, goolayool): waterholing tree

goolara: moonlight

goolawa: yesterday

goola-willeel[5] (goolah-willeel): topknot pigeon

goolay[5]**:** string bag

goolay-yali[5] (goolayyahlee): pelican

goolee: sand lizard

goolmarry[6]**:** shield

gooloo[5]**:** magpie

goomai[5]**:** water rat

goombeelga[5] (goombeelgah): canoe made of bark

goomble-gubbon[5]**:** bustard turkey

goomilla[5] (goomillah): woman's garment made of string; girl's garment with belt of possum sinews, with woven possum hair strands in front, about a foot square

goonagulla (goonagullah): sky

goonai[5] (goohnai): death wail

goonama: snow

goonaroo: whistling duck

goonarook: wood duck

goonawarra: swan

goonbar[3]**:** he, it, she

goonbean[5]**:** sweet excretions on the bibbil tree

goon-der-rah[6]**:** fight (verb)

goondie: see gunyah

goondnomda: water flowing over rocks

goondooi: see gundooi
goondool: stringybark tree
goongkoong[4]**:** nose
goongwar[3]**:** this
goonnear: carpet snake
goonur[5]**:** kangaroo rat
goorewon: tabooed woman
goori[5]**:** fat; tree
goornan: heat
goornung: see gunyang
gooroondoodilbaydilbay: south wind
goorung: fireplace
goorunna[2]**:** good
gootagoodo[8]**:** heart
gooweera[5]**:** pointing bone
gora: long
goroke[4]**:** magpie
goug gour gahgah, gougourgahgah, and **gourgourgahgah:** see goo-goor-gaga
Gowa-gay[5] **(Gowargay):** The Coalsack, which is the Emu in the Milky Way
gowdalie: hardwood fishing spear
goyarra[1, 6]**:** sand
grantali[2]**:** big
grauwe: large
grauwe ru: larger
grauwun[2]**:** bury
gree[4]**:** canoe
grokumbalin[2]**:** stamp
grooee: see gruee
gruee[5] **(grooee):** tree with bitter fruit
guana[5]**:** me
gubba[5]**:** good
gubbera[5] **(gubberah):** crystals; clear stones used for magical purposes
gudda[5] **(guddah):** red lizard

gudjal[1]**:** two
gudjal-gudjal[1]**:** four
gudjyt[1] **(gudjyt barrab):** heavens
gue[5]**:** blood
guie[5]**:** mine
guiebet: see gweebet
guineeboo: see gwai-nee-bu
guliba[5]**:** three
gulle: go up
gullee: see gulli
gulleemeah: see gulli-maya
gulli[5] **(gullee):** water
gulli-maya[5] **(gulleemeah):** water bag
gumalkoolin[4]**:** willy wagtail
gummy: spear
gunbower: tortuous, winding
gundai: see gunyah
gundar yuro[6]**:** cloud
gundoo[5] **(goondooi, gundooee):** solitary emu
gunee: mother
gunmarl[5]**:** taboo; place where someone has died
gunni[5] **(gunnai, gunnee):** digging stick, yam stick
gununo[6]**:** black snake
gunyah[5] **(goondie, gundai):** hut, bark shelter
gun-yu-mu[5] **(gunyahmoo, gunyahnoo):** east wind
gunyang (goornung): kangaroo apple
gun-yanni[5]**:** tree
gurburra[5] **(gurburrah):** north
gurdar[1]**:** two
guridjadu[6]**:** carpet snake
gurkuk[4]**:** blood
gurra[2]**:** east; south-west
gurra malye[2]**:** south-west wind
gurraymi[5] **(gurraymy):** woman's name for gayandi, q.v.

gwabba[1]: good
gwai[5]: red
Gwai-billa[5] (Gwai-billah): Mars (the red star)
gwai-nee-bu[5] (guineboo, gwineeboo): robin redbreast
gwandalan: peace, quiet, rest
gweebet[5] (guiebet): thorny creeper with edible fruit
gweeon[6] (gwheh-un): stone tomahawk
gwineeboo: see gwai-nee-bu
gyn[1]: one

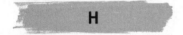

halcoppatunein[8]: sick
hanya[6]: stone
harnakar[2] (haranekar): these
Harrimiah: mythical black goanna
hatarear-amalla[8]: frightened
heeterra[8]: gum tree
hetarracadin[8]: pull
hetrala[8]: lazy
hii hii[2] (hiau hiau): any
hikkai[2] (hik): immediately, just now; this
hikkai nungge[2]: today
hillimung: shield
hill-lee[8]: fig
hillta[8]: hut
himbing: see humpy
hipmilta[8]: mirage
hokarra[8]: married woman
holanyee[8]: cry (verb)
holcoppa-tunein[8]: vein
holemunda (olemunda): dust
holtar[8]: stick
hong-gar[8]: reed
hontee: neck
hooray[8] (hooroo): hair

hotooworry[8]: cloud
humpy (himbing, oompi, yamba): bark shelter or hut
hundoeta[8]: see undooeata
hungappa[8]: crow
hungiaquar: hungry
hurramira[8]: goanna

ianuk[3]: I
ibi[2]: breast
icherramal[8]: shoot (verb)
idudar bungaru[1]: girl
igeelu[2]: father
igera[2]: mother
ignum: fall (verb)
ijawu[3]: fish
ikkati: sit
il[2] (ile): by
ilbanda[3]: earth
ilchar-atnitta[8]: hand
ildmurra[8]: dew
illa-illa[5]: no, not
illcarrie[8]: sky
illcha[8]: finger
illdo-malla[8]: cut (verb)
illginga: beefwood tree
illgulldenem: kick (verb)
ill-lamanoo[8]: long way
ill-loong[8] (ill-looka): dead
ill-lua[8]: salt
ill-luaquasha[8]: salt water
ill-lulta[8]: march fly
illpellpa: grass for thatching
illperippa[8]: leaf
illpilla: eyelash
illpun: along
illyer-manda[8]: ring
iluka: near the sea
ilumba: Moreton Bay ash

imba[2]: skin
imbunga[8]: cooked
imbye[8]: leave (verb)
imuran[3]: big
in anyril[2]: for him
inberra: shallow
incarnie[8]: laugh
indarnie[8]: frown
indenima: splinter
inger: foot, hoof
inger-godill[8]: horse
ingitja (ingitsa): new moon
ingualmulbil: foot
ingwa[8]: duck
injaracna: sneeze
injeer-mayjeer[8]: mist
injerima: breath
injerima unditta[8]: offensive breath
inkata: elder, wise man
inna[5]: this
innar-linger[8]: echidna
inntoo[8]: fur
interlina: shoe
intinne: necklace
intulka[8]: stubborn
inye[2]: also
inyeppa[8]: navel
inyerra-alcrim: shame
iona[3]: fire; tree
iperta: geranium; hole
ipminger[8]: altogether
ipoque[3]: cold
ippeeculca[8]: teat
ira[3] (jara): eyes
irinka[8]: dog
irita[8]: deaf
irriakura: edible tuber
irtaie[6]: giant nettle
irtalie: bean tree
ita[6]: scrub; swamp fish
iterika[8]: green
iterra[2]: be quick, run!

itickera[8]: root
itichika[8]: red
itichika: see ititika
ititika (itichika): blanket
ityan[2]: him
itye[2]: outside
itye[2]: see kitye
iwadi[3]: head
iwala[3]: man
iyebana[6]: peewit
iyoura[8]: echo
iyouta[3]: spinifex

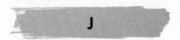

J

jaanga[4]: hut
jabiru: stork. It appears that this word has been imported into the aboriginal vocabulary from South America. The same word is used for the saddle-bill in Central Africa. In Australia it has also appeared in legend in the form djabiru
jackaroo (jackeroo): name for a young squatter, probably coming from the word tchaceroo, q.v., or from 'Jacky Raw' a 'new chum' on the analogy of the kangaroos
jalamari[3]: ears
jamida[3]: mouth
jane[4]: foot
janga[3]: foot
jara[3]: see ira
jarrah[1]: tree and timber known variously as blue gum, mahogany gum, and swamp mahogany. It is a corruption of the native word jerryhl. It is known only as jarrah in

Western Australia, where it is native, and throughout the rest of Australia, where 'jarrah' is a familiar timber noted for its durability

jeeba: springtime corrobboree
Jeedara: large mythical water snake
jeetho: leave (verb)
jellan⁴: tongue
jeni³: nose
jenna⁴: foot
jenning-gherrie: willy wagtail
jenoong: foot
jerambitty yarka⁴: spear
jerilderie: place where reeds grow
jerron and **jerrund:** see jirrand
jerryhl: see jarrah
jewang⁴: star
jidi¹: rain
jigi³: hand; teeth
jil-crow-a-berry: corruption of the aboriginal name for rat-tail grass
jilmil³: nose
jimara³: hair
jimari: stone knife
jimba: see jombock
Jimbun: spirit that controls love affairs
jimiramira³: big
jinang⁴: foot
jinchilla⁶: cypress pine
jindivik: destroy, lose
jinkana²: give
jinna: foot
jirra⁴: kangaroo
jirra: another term for dilli, q.v.
jirrand⁵ (jerron, jerrund): afraid; fear
jirriman⁴: knee
jitcha⁸: no

joatgba⁴: kangaroo
jombock (dombock, dumbog, jimba): white clouds or mist which precede rain
jorrer⁸: shin
jumbuck: sheep. A corruption of jombock, q.v. When the aboriginals first saw sheep they compared them to white clouds
jumbunna: talk together
jumjum⁴: bellbird

K

kaain: see aya
kaandha: whale
kaar: white cockatoo
kabatang⁴: moon
kabbera: see cobbra
kabbin⁴: cold
kabbulin²: mock
kabee²: see cobbie
kabu²: three
kabura: see cobbra
kadaitcha: evil
kaddely⁵ (kuddelee): dog
kadee³: mother
kaga⁶: water hole
kagailya²: hair
kagil⁵: bad
kahar²: root of tree
kaiaking²: tongue
kaidundun²: shout
kai hai: an expression of approval, equivalent to Encore! Hear! Hear!
kaiher⁴: spear
kaikai²: light (adj); plain (noun)
kaike: reed spear
kaikundun² (kaikulun): call (verb)
kaingani²: young man

kaintyamande[2]: bladder
kaiya[6]: spear with several stingray barbs
kakalan[6]: chicken hawk
kakee[5]: this
kaki[2]: bough
kakie[5]: that
kakke[6]: blood
kakowera: tree fern
kakuri: dry
kalajah[3] (alajah): ears
kalangbool[2]: swamp with many red gums
kalbe: pillow
kaldari[2]: tail
kalde[2]: language; throat; windpipe
kaldow[2] (kaldowinyeri, klauo, klauoanyeri): a long time ago, old
kaldowamp[2]: always, continually, ever
kalduke: bunch of feathers; umbilical cord
kalk[4]: tree
kalkerri[2]: liver
kalkkalk[4]: club
kalkree[5]: midday
kalkro[5]: jagged spear
kalla[1]: fire
kallakkure[2]: island
kallang[1]: heat
kallarak[1]: heat
kallarroo[1]: path leading to water
kalletulik[3]: two
kalparrin[2]: help carry a load
kalperri[2]: shoveller duck
kalpulun[2] (kalpundun): wink
kaltee[5]: emu
kalti[2]: spear
kaltin[2]: dig
kalun[6]: one
kalyan[2]: here; stop (verb)

kam[6]: head
kama[4]: spear
kamaroo[8]: uncle
kamballa[5]: young woman
kambara[6]: crocodile
kambera[5]: father
kambie[5]: garment
kambigo[4]: night
kameruka[5]: wait till I return
kami[5]: prickly lizard
kampa[6]: messmate tree
kan[2]: them
kana[6]: spear
kanake: fighting club, waddy
kanakie[5]: water vessel
kanamer[4]: heat
kanawinkie[5]: tomorrow
kanbigur mel[1]: eye
kandara[5] (carndarah, kandora): blood
kandari[2]: rope
kandauwe[2]: their
kandeer: branch
kandelka[5]: good
kandora[5]: see kandara
kaneky[5]: yellow-crested cockatoo
kangaroo: the famous animal which leaps on its hind legs, balances itself by its tail, and carries its young in a pouch. There has been much debate as to whether it is an aboriginal word, and many explanations have been given. There is no doubt that it was not used to any great extent by the blackfellows in the early days of settlement, for they regarded it as an English word. It was first recorded in 1770 when H.M.S. *Endeavour* was at Cooktown, but fifteen years

later it was not known to the aborigines of New South Wales. One explanation is that the word means 'I don't know', but no similar sounding word or words with this meaning have been recorded.

kangernackie[5]: this side

kanggen[2]: laugh at

kangkin[2]: laugh

kangnarra: sweat (verb)

kan-guama[5]: sweat

kangulandah[2]: again, first, once more

kangulun[2]: another, other

kangulun nungge[2]: day before yesterday

kaning marrewan[4]: throwing stick

kanku[2]: boy

kanow[4]: he, it, she

kanpuka[4]: white water-lily

kantarli[2]: sweat (noun)

kaoga[5]: head

kaooroo: water-lily

kaoota[7]: dusk, evening

kapo[5]: silence

kappa[6]: moon

kappara: see cobbra

kappin[2]: mock

kar[2]: they

Kara: spider woman

karagata: umbrella bush

kara kara: gold

Karakarock (Kararock, Kur-ruk-ar-ook): goddess, daughter of Pund-jel

karangkarang[4]: hair

karawun: long leaf used for making baskets

karbeethong: laughter

karbolquar[3]: mouth

kardidi baldin[1]: small

kardingoola: midday, noon

kardo[1]: see kerdo

kare[5]: man

kargaruk[4] (kurruk): sand

kari[2]: smoke

karinga: today

karinye[2]: mother-in-law

karkalla: pigface

karkaro[5]: spear

karkarook: sand

karlo[2]: immediately, just now

karlowan[2]: behind, second

karlowan atye[2]: last, final

karlowun[2]: turn around

karlye[2]: crab

karndobara[4]: blood

karnick[4]: throwing stick

karobran: together

karoom: native currant

karraba: cut (verb)

karragain: stone tomahawk

karraka[5]: leg

karraninke[5]: day

karranga: up

karri (kari): eucalypt

karrit[4]: rain

karte[2]: island

karthro[5]: there

karu: spear with stone head

karumba: soul or spirit of an old man

karwin: grass tree

kaso[5]: another

kata[6]: mother

katan[6]: cut (verb)

katata[4]: cold

katee-wailwo[5]: small

kathowart[4]: you

katoa[5]: short

katta[1]: head; hill

kattamangara[1]: hair

kattidj[1]: hear

kattik[1]: night
katya[6]: far away
katye[4]: heat
katyil[2]: yes
katyin[4]: water
kauerti[2]: swan
kaukau[2]: bless, thank
kauwul[5]: big
kaya: uncle
kayannie[4]: water
ke[2] (keh): eh!
kearka[8]: bowerbird
keda[2]: boomerang
kehla nyauwe[4]: day
keilambete: brackish lake
kein[6]: moon
kekuyan[6]: spiny ant-eater
kelgalli[2]: infant
kelgelli[2]: caterpillar
keli[4]: dog
kelunji: galah bird
kembla: abundant
kena[6]: fresh water crocodile
kendi: lizard; mythical frilled
    lizard
kene[2]: firestick
kenggun[2] (kengk): they two
keni[2] (kene): cinders; ember
kenkank[2]: grey-haired
kenkulun[2] (kenk): grey
kerau kiath[2]: above
kerdo[1] (kardo): husband, wife,
    spouse
kerlpa[5]: knot
kerlpra[5]: finger
kertum[4]: boomerang
kertun[2]: bend (intrans. verb)
ketchum[4]: hut
keyakki[2]: five
keyap[4]: one
kia[2]: spear
kiambram: dense forest

kiar[4]: bad
kiata: heat; summer
kibulyo: whistling duck
kiewa: sweet water
kielpa[5]: short distance
kikinummi[2]: black snake
kiley[1] (kyli, kylie): type of
    boomerang
kilkie: water hen
kilkilyalin[2]: destroy, scatter; rub
    (verb)
kilkulun[2]: smooth
killara: permanent
kilpa[2]: cool, cold
kilpalie: cold
kilpanie: winter
kilto[5]: grassy
kimba[5]: bush fire
kimmuli (kimmule): teatree
kin[2]: him
kinankurnunk[2]: day after
kinauwe[2] (kinauwurle): his
kindyerra: grass
kindilan[6]: joyful
kine[4]: fish
kinedana[5]: laugh (verb)
kineman[4] (kinemin): black
kineyah: rice
kinga[4]: he, it, she
kinie-ger: native cat
kinka: laugh
kinkindele[2]: tortoise, turtle
kinkuna: laugh (verb)
kinma[4]: this
kinma[6]: awake
kinner[5]: they
kinpin[2]: sweet
kinyet[4]: they
kirkuwe[2]: itch (verb)
kirli[2]: coot
kirra[6]: leaf
kirrang: wattle

kirrkie: whistling hawk
kirrpiyirrka: seagull
kitye[2] (atye, itye): he, it, she
klallin[2]: fiery hot, scald, thirsty
klallin ruwe[2]: parched ground
klare[2]: short-tailed goanna
klartin[2]: shine
klauo: see kaldow
kldeimindin[2]: fetch
koa[2]: crow
koala (colac, colah, colo, coola, kool-la): native bear
koala[3]: man
kobbera: see cobbra
kobi: medicine man
kobra: see cobbra
kobul: see cobbra
koiranah: eagle
kodala[6]: reed
koiyung[5]: fire
koka[2]: see kukaa
kokate[2]: see kukathe
kokereka[5]: black
kokeri[5]: hut
kokipijira[6]: rain, storm
koko[5]: see kokora
kokora[4]: rain
kokora[5] (koko): head
kolet[6]: dove
kolge[2] (kilgi): she-oak
kolkon[4]: boy
kollah[5]: tree
kolle: water
kolora: fresh water lagoon
kolya[5]: winter
kombona[5]: old woman
komlia[5]: big
konak[3]: earth
konamba[4]: woman
konda: cabbage tree
kondarle[2]: whale
kondu[4]: club

konegerana[5]: sulky
kong[6]: water
kongaroo[8]: sister
kongoola[2]: fresh water fish
kongwak: catch (verb)
koninderie[5]: rainbow
konk[2]: away
konkaer[6]: head
konkea: aunt
konkinyeri[2]: alone, apart
konkon[6]: white fish hawk
konkonbah[2]: hunt (noun)
konkuwarrin[2]: send
konnung: man-killing stick
konol[3]: sky
koobah: see coobah
koob-bor: native bear
Koobooboodgery: night spirit
kooberry: bidyan ruffe (fresh water fish), also called silver perch or bream
kooding[3]: mother
koodnapina: brown duck
Koodyoorinadyal[6]: Southern Cross
koo-ee-lung: porpoise
kooim[4]: kangaroo
kooka: animal food, flesh, game
kookaburra (goburra, gogobera): laughing jackass
koola[2] (koolar[6]): kangaroo
koolein: man
koolena: sandy plain
kooliman: see coolamon
koolin[4]: man
koolkuna: protect
kool-la: see koala
koolyangarra: children
koolyer[5]: cold
koolyn: black swan
koolootaroo: magpie lark
koombar[6]: bark

koomeela: fly (verb)

koonappoo: mouse

koondi[5]**:** hut

koongarra: noise of the flight of birds when rising from the ground

koongarra[8] **(koongarroo):** kangaroo

koongawa[4]**:** good

koongoora: elder sister

koongun: scorpion

koon-ja-gilbee[8]**:** old woman

koonje[5]**:** camp

koonkie: doctor

koonthooi: kelp

koonwarra[4]**:** oyster

koora[2]**:** day

kooraba[4]**:** blood

koorala: walk (verb)

kooraltha: spotted ferret

koorang: snake

kooranya: other daughters

koorngoo: food bag

koornkoo[2]**:** camp

koorong[4]**:** canoe

kooronya: myself

kooroorook: stick

koorowar[3]**:** water

koorowera: black diver

koorpa: flood

koorrnong: creek which dries up in summer

koort-boork boork: grove of she-oak trees

koortgang: speckled teal

kooruck: soil

koorunga: four

kootopan[4]**:** one

kooya[2] **(kuya):** fish

koppie[2]**:** see cobbie

kopulun[2]**:** avoid a weapon thrust

kor[4]**:** sea

kora[6]**:** native companion

koradji[5] **(coradgee):** clever man, medicine man, sorcerer

korana[3]**:** see orana

kore[2]**:** woman

korne[2]**:** man

korneok: whistling duck

korobra: dance (verb)

korowalkin[2]**:** lie on the back

korpi[6]**:** mangrove

korra[2]**:** grass

korraco[8]**:** red ochre

korrorook: stork

korrumburra: blowfly

koruldambi[2]**:** white owl

kotbityerowe[2]**:** bull ant

kotla[2]**:** tail

kotyap[4]**:** stone

kow[4]**:** nose

kowa[5]**:** plenty

kowallong-cowling: outside place

kowandi[2]**:** smoke signal

kowan worang[4]**:** head

kowia[5]**:** come here

kowinka: red mangrove

kowundun[2]**:** step (verb)

koyunga: plain surrounded by forest

koynaratingana[7]**:** sandy beach

kraiyelin[2]**:** jealous

kralin[2]**:** bury

krambruk: landing place

krambruk[4]**:** sandy place

kranalang: crab

krangnark[4]**:** hill

krepauwe[2]**:** bread

kringgun[2]**:** grow

kringyang: sand mullet

kroman[6]**:** kangaroo

krowalle[2]**:** blue crane

krugarupe[2]**:** oven

krunkun[2]**:** name (verb)

kruwalde[2]: bloody
kruwe[2] (krui): blood
kua[6]: dingo
kuarun[2] (kuun): distant
kuboin[4]: scrub pigeon
kuddelee[2]: see kaddely
kudgee: castor oil plant
kudla[2] (kurla): fire
kuging-cudgen: red pigment
kukaa[2] (koka): head
kukabuka[2]: die
kukai[6]: mother's older brother
kukathe[2] (kokate): orphan
kuke[2]: elbow
kukki[6]: blood
kuk kuk ki[2]: five
kula: bloodwood tree
kulagook[3]: one
kulai: echidna
kulan[6]: possum
kulde[2]: farm; froth; saliva
kuldi[2]: mate
kuldoo: edible seed
kulduke[2]: doctor
kuldun[2]: see kulkun
kulgarnie[2]: hot wind
kulgulankin[2]: see kulyulaikin
kulgutye[2]: motherless
kulka[2]: star
kulkawura: afternoon
kulk turring[4]: tree
kulkuldi[2]: crooked
kulkulook: fishing net
kulkun[2] (kuldun): burn (scorch), scorch
kulla (kullah): native bear
kullack[4]: club
kulletulik-kulagook[3]: three
kullin[4]: throwing stick
kullun[2]: pliable
kulmul[4]: blood
kuloomba: native clover

kulpana[5] (kulpanah): speak
kultha[5]: another
kultown[5]: duck
kulu: seed
kulyulaikin[2] (kulgulankin): ashamed
kuma[2]: see cooma
kumala[6]: mud shell
kumalie[5]: small duck
kumaloro: sign language
kumarie[6]: blood
kumbargang myardack[1]: night
kumbelin[2]: sweetness
kumbi[5] (comebee, cumbee): kangaroo skin bag
kumbokumbo: death dance of warriors
kumbooran[5]: east
kumbu[5] (comeboo, comebo): stone tomahawk
kumbumbana[5]: a number of women
kummaiyem[2]: distant
kummun[2]: deep
kumpa[2]: urine
kumpun[2]: blow (verb), blow the fire
kuna[5]: grey hair
kunabinjelu[2]: mosquito
kunakuna[5]: box tree
kunakunakasno[5]: bark (verb)
kunar[2]: excrement
kunara[6]: tiger shark
kunarle[2]: emu feathers
kunda[6]: dog
kunda: decorated digging stick
kundart: cloud
kundemer[4]: mouth
kunden[2]: kiss; rest
kundgulde: butterfish
kundolo[4]: eye
kundy[5]: mosquito

kunewallin mewe[2]: cross (ill-
tempered)
kung[6]: water
kunga[4]: make
kunga-gnarra[5]: throat
kungenyeriwallin[2]: epileptic fit
kungkungullun[2] (kungkung-
under): love (verb)
kunkungundun[2]: loved
kung our[2]: listen!
kungullin[2]: think
kungun[2]: hear, understand
kungyuttulun[2]: eat greedily
kuniekoondie: crayfish
kunkulde[2]: Murray mouth sprat
kunkun[2]: swallow (verb)
kunnai[6]: spear
kunnan-beili[5] (cunnembeille,
cunnunbeille): Baiame's
second wife; pigweed root
kunnie: jew lizard
kunnogwurra[3]: canoe
kuntnama-cuerana[5]: smile
(verb)
kunthold[2]: gladness, joy
kunthun[2]: glad
kuntun[2]: blaze (verb)
kuntyan[6]: pandanus
kuntyari: plant with edible roots
kunye[2]: enough
kupa: white man
kupala[6]: white
kuppa: water
kur[2]: calf (of leg); river
kuracca: white-crested cockatoo
kuranye[2]: closely woven
kur-bo-roo: native bear
kurda[2]: man
kurdaitcha (coordaitcha,
goditcha): shoes made of emu
feathers, pointed at both ends
so that trackers cannot tell

which way the wearer has
gone. The term is applied to
the shoes by the white man,
but by the aborigine to the
wearer, who is usually being
hunted by a vengeful enemy
kure[2]: neck
kurla[2]: see kudla
kurla[2]: wood
kurle[2]: head
kurmoonah[6]: honey
kurnkuni[2]: relative
kurra: fierce storm, gale
kurragong: shade tree
kurrajong[5] (currajong): tree
Sterlucia (also called noonga);
also used of fibrous plants
kurrara: place frequented by
possums
kurramilla: a small pink shell
kurrawa: rough sea
kurrawan: reed
kurreah: see kurria
kurrengk[2]: see tarrukengk
kurria [5] (kurreah): crocodile; also
the name of the corcodile who
lives in the Milky Way
kurrin[2]: ask
kurrin[5]: sand
kurrinyerengk[2]: trousers
kurrnung: small creek
kur-rook-ar-rook: koala with
young
kurrowera: shag
kurruk[4]: see kargaruk
Kur-ruk-ar-ook: see Karakarock
kurrung[4]: big
kurta[2]: excrement
kurtli: she-oak
kurtoo[2]: wife
kurunkun[2]: blow (of wind)
kurunto[5]: belly

kur-ur-rook: native companion
kutha[2]**:** club
kuti[2]**:** cockle
kutjara[2]**:** ear
kutkuti[2]**:** crooked
kutsha[2]**:** another, more
kutta yang[4]**:** head
kutthara[2]**:** see godarra
kutyeri[2]**:** thin
kutyo[2]**:** small
kuun[2]**:** see kuarun
ku-utyun[2]**:** far
kuwullun[2]**:** stick (verb)
kuya[2]**:** see kooya
kuyan[2]**:** honey bee
kuyulpi[2]**:** parrot
kwa[5]**:** dance of the crows
kwaky[4]**:** day
kwimpy[6]**:** kangaroo
Kwoolcudee: lizard god
kyeema[4]**:** kangaroo
kyeema: dawn
kyena: barracoota
kyli and **kylie:** see kiley
kynkar[1]**:** father

laane-coore (lanacoora): home of the kangaroo
laane-pyramul: home of the emu
laap: see lerp
lakebi[2]**:** few, small number
lakkari[2]**:** honeysuckle tree
lakkin[2]**:** throw a spear
laldilald[2]**:** round about
lalirra[3]**:** sun
lal-lal: small quantity of water
lamaldar[2] (maldamaldar): curl (noun)
lamaliala[3]**:** mouth

lamangurk[4]**:** girl
lamgalio[3]**:** small
lamilla[3]**:** stone
lammin[2]**:** carry on the back
lanacoora: see laane-coore
lane[4]**:** good
langi: dwelling place
langi-dorn: bellbird nest
langi-gherim: home of the yellow-tailed black kangaroo
langi-giran: nest of the black cockatoo
langmong[4]**:** stone
lanyalin[2]**:** fester
lapoinya[7]**:** tree fern
lar[4]**:** hut
larayelarra[3]**:** hair
larelar[2]**:** circular, round
lare muntunt[2]**:** on the other side; upside down
lark[4]**:** cloud
larolk[3]**:** fire; tree
lawitbari[3]**:** two
lawitbarimot[3]**:** three
lea (leang, leanyook): tooth
leawill[4] (langeel, leangeel, leanguel, leeangle, leawil, le-ow-el): wooden club bent at the head. The name leeangle is probably half aboriginal and half European, the 'angle' referring to the bent head, but bearing a resemblance to the aboriginal word
leeang[4]**:** teeth
leemurra[3]**:** eye
leena[7]**:** possum
leetunger[3]**:** fire
leewin[2]**:** bend (intrans verb)
leita[3]**:** small
leongatha[4]**:** tooth
leripma: flame

lermalner[3]: hair
lerp[4] (laap, leurp): sweet; manna secreted by an insect
lerra[8]: river
lerunna: flounder
lewurmi[2]: buttocks
lianwill[4]: club
licka[8]: prickle
lidjet: fish
lielu: husband
likoo[2]: canoe
likoorler[3]: spear
lilla[8]: gravel
lilliri[2]: shade, shadow
lillkar[8]: wind
lilyerwer[3]: hill
limga[3]: stone
lintyeri[2]: young root of weeds
lirok[4]: woman
lirralirra: wren
lirt[4]: hair
liyer[3]: fish
loa (lowa): woman
loaranneleah: blue sky
loilyer[3]: moon
lokkin kaye[2]: make a basket
lokulun[2]: howl (dog)
lokure[2]: mussel
loldu[2]: down in; go; go down
lom[2]: you two
lomar[3]: ears
longerenong: dividing of the waters
loongootpar[3]: kangaroo
loombark: water grass
loongana[7]: swift
looranah: brushwood
loorapa: caught
loorea[3]: moon
loorl[3]: sit down
loru[2] (moru): ascend, go up
lottheggi[2]: bat

lowalde[2]: summer
lowan[2, 4]: scrub turkey, native pheasant or mallee fowl
lowana[7]: girl
lowanna[7]: beauty
lowralarree[3]: we
lubra[7]: woman
luderick (ludrick): black-fish
luk[2] (lun): as, like
lukun[2]: sour
lulur[2]: broken
lurki[2]: lizard
luwun[2] (lulun-intrans. form): break
luwun-turtangk[2]: kneel
lyaleetea[7]: sea
lyeltya: breakers

M

ma[3]: eye, see
maa[4]: eye
Maamu: leader of evil spirits
mabingi mulko[1]: cloud
mackunya[5]: turn over
macooloma[7]: draw, paint
madba[3]: kangaroo
madbarra[3]: tree
madhi[5] (mahthi): dog
madlanchi[2]: bad
mado[5]: trumpeter-perch, bleak
magra: pouch or sling in which women carry their children
mague[5]: eyebrow
magul[6]: head
mah[5]: totem; brand; hand
mahmak[4]: father
mahn: long
mahrung[4]: see
mahthi : see madhi
mai: fruit and vegetables, food

maiatta[6]: sugar-bag
maigamaigwa: thumb
maimah: see mayama
mai-ra[5]: paddymelon
mairn[4]: heavens
maitlia[2]: clay
maiya[6]: vegetable food
maiyanowe[2]: grand-mother (paternal)
maiyarare[2]: grand-child (father's side)
maiyingar[2] (maiyinggar): cloak, garment, possessions
maka: small fire
make[2]: cheek
makga[5]: doctor
maki: hunting boomerang
makkin[2]: pick up
mako: edible wood grub
makoo: cloud
makoro[5]: fish
mal[5]: one
malangenna[7]: infant
malbooma[6]: wind
maldamaldar[2]: see lamaldar
malde[2]: foreign, strange, different
maleye[5]: husband
mali[4]: he, it, she
mali: non-material form of both human beings and inanimate objects
malie[5]: man
malkin[2]: creep
mallana[7]: canoe
mallanbool[4]: pool with reeds
mallee[4]: scrub of dwarf eucalypts
maller[4]: throwing stick
malloomar[3]: head
mallowe: Murray mouth salmon
malpuri[2]: guilty of murder
maltaiar[2] (malde, malte): few, some

maltthi[2]: night
malunna[7]: nest
malyar[2]: flock
mam[2]: animal food, meat
mama[6]: hold, pick up
mamalla[3]: star
Mamaragan: the lightning man
mamarap[1]: man
mambamya pumo[5]: widow
mambo[5]: sister-in-law
mame[2]: fish
mamiliri[3]: hand
mamma[2] (mamman): father
mammal[1]: boy
mamman[1]: see mamma
mammart[1]: sea
mammerool[3]: dog
mamook[4]: father
mamun[3]: tree
mana[6]: neck, run
manai[2]: see mani
manamana[4]: hand
manar[2]: fin
manba[5] (wanga): flesh
mandigara[1]: girl
mandurama[5]: water hole
manenee[3]: hand
maneroo: plain
mangaroo: phalanger, flying squirrel
manga tandra[2]: head
mangka[6]: behind
mangnoo[2]: rain
mani[2] (manai): equal
manillirra[3]: hut
manity[3]: sun
mankara[2] (munkara): girl
mankuri[2]: belly, stomach
manna[7]: wattle tree
manninkki[2]: leech
mant[2]: gently, slowly
mantaba[6]: bustard

manya[6]: small
manyeekerrik[3]: spear
mao-warang: native pepper tree
mapa[6]: flap (verb)
mar[3]: cloud
maragajang[4]: small
marandoo[4]: plenty
marangane[2]: crowd (verb)
marangani[2]: autumn
maranowe[2]: elder sister
maratulde[2]: empty
marauwe[2]: sister
maray[5]: pilchard
marbangye[2]: black diver
marbeangrook: evening star
maremuntunt[2]: beneath, inside
marhra[1]: hand
mari: wallaby
marila[6]: man
markrah[5]: dark
markulde[2] (markulli): shoulder,
  shoulder blade
marloo: pipeclay; kangaroo
marloorie[8]: claypan
marloorie-buntor[8]: lake
marma[8]: sore
marman[4]: father
marmingatha: prayer
Marmoo[8]: demon spirit
marnditye[2]: because
marngowi[2]: sugar
marnmin[2]: beat (verb)
maroo[4]: pine tree
maroong (mahrung, maron): pine
  tree
marpanye[2]: club
marra[2]: see murra
marram: kangaroo
marro: instruction of initiates
marrongie: spear shaft
marroo[8]: black
marte[2]: stone

marti[2]: limestone, rock
matari[2]: man
matong: great, strong
mattini: double-pointed club
matyimuk[4]: wife
maunanyuk[4]: hand
mawiliri[3]: teeth
may[5] (mayr): wind
mayama[5] (maimah): stone
Maya-mayi[5] (Meamei): the
  Pleiades (the seven sisters)
mayra[5]: (mayrah): spring wind
mbal[3]: hair
mea[6]: eye; open mesh
mealler[4]: husband
Meamei: see Maya-mayi
meangener[3]: man
mearann[8]: call (verb)
meauke[2]: crayfish
meekyluka: Sturt's desert pea
meelitshel[3]: small
meelugger[3]: woman
meetawarri: old woman
mega[1]: moon
melape[2]: devil, evil spirit
meli[2]: company of people
melinya[5]: fingernail
melkin[2]: shade (verb)
mell[1]: eye
memerangi: cough
mempin[2]: beat, kill, strike
menaikulun[2]: turn inside out
menaikundun[2]: bend (trans.
  verb)
menamenakarin[2]: roll (verb)
menane[2]: penis
menarte[2]: blunt
menbi[2]: fat
mendemullar[6]: nose
mendic: sick
mendin[2]: fight (verb)
mendolo[5]: nose

menengi[2]: mud
mengye[2]: how; whose
meningkundun[2]: bow
menmenengkuri[2]: martin, swallow
menperre[2]: frog
menurte[2]: short
mera[5]: string bag
meralde[2]: spear with quartz head
meraldi[2]: dried, withered
meralke[2]: tree root
meralte[2]: boat
merammin[2]: see nammin
merate[2]: bare, naked
merbuck[4]: cold
merendamin[2]: drink (verb)
merippin[2]: cut (verb)
merkani[2]: strange, wild
merkawatyeri[2]: riddled with holes
merke[2] (merki): hole, small hole
merlaga[5]: the other side
mermawer mokiter[3]: die
Merpulla: rain woman
merrenetta: see murrandudda
merri[4]: stone
merrican-kein[6]: moon
merrina: deceit, pretence
merringannee[5]: south wind
meta[2]: land
metpadinger[3]: club
mewe[2]: bowels
mewultun[2]: want (verb)
meya[6]: lift
mi[6]: eye
mia[2]: sleep
mia[5]: cold
miah[1]: moon
miailler[4]: eye
miala[2]: sleep (verb)
miam[4]: hut
mia-mia: hut, shelter

mian[4]: wife
mianameena[7]: pool
Mickibri: messenger of the bird goddess Nulgin
mickie[5]: quick
middip[3]: live (verb)
midgee[8]: blood
midjee[5]: species of acacia tree
midjeer[5]: barbed stick for prising grubs out of crevices
midna[2] (mina): eye; see
mie[5]: girl
miga[6]: dog
miintinta[6]: sea turtle
mije: little
miki[1]: moon
mikurri[2]: spotted bandicoot
mil[5]: eye
milbung: blind (literally eye dead)
milki[2]: eye
milkurli[2]: orange (colour)
millair and millear: see millia
milla milla[6]: baby
millemurro: pelican
millia[5] (millair, millear): kangaroo rat
millin[2]: bewitch, charm (verb), sorcery
millin-dulu-nubba[5] (millindooloonubbah): bird
milling-kalla[6]: four
milloo: river
milo[6]: eye
milpara (milpera): company
miltee[8]: nail
milterree[5]: stiffness
milyali: infant
milyali tinyeri[2]: offspring
milyarm[1]: star
milyaroo: dusk
mimbo[8]: water vessel

mina[2]: see midna
minamberang: clematis
minar: mark
minarto[5]: what name
mincarlie[8]: rain
mind[2] (mindenanyir): why
minderin[4]: hair
mindi[6]: teeth
mindi (myndie): bunyip-snake
mindyah[6]: cloud
minga[2]: ill, illness, pain, sick, sickness
minga[5]: hole in the ground, well
minga[8]: small black ant
minga: bad
Mingara: good spirit which controls the clouds
ming-ari (min-jin, minn-narie): mountain devil
mingga[5] (minggah): spirit-haunted tree
miningkar[2]: worm
minkie[5]: daylight
minna: beach; what; wrist
minnear: see myrna
minninger[3]: night
minn-narie[8]: mountain devil
minnta[8]: shadow
minntin: pinch (verb)
mintambi[2]: string
mintchie[6]: foot
minti[2]: small portion
minya[2]: small
minyai[2] (munyarai): how many?
minyaka: tomorrow
minyandai[2]: how often?
minyun[4]: kangaroo
miowera[4]: emu
mirambeek: mine
mirimp[2]: half
miriyan[6]: star
mirla[2]: throwing stick

mirnyong[4, 7] (mirrnyong): midden containing shells
miro[1]: throwing stick
mirpin[2]: sink (verb)
mirr[4]: eye
mirramirildin[2] (mirramerildin): decayed, rotten, withered
mirreen: south
mirria[5] (mirrieh): polygonum shrub
mirrin[5] : cloud
mirror[8]: country
mirru[6]: wife
mirrung[6]: girl
mirta[2]: white ant
mitamit: speed
mittagong: small mountain
mityak[4]: rain
mityan[4]: moon
mitye[2]: name
miyer[6]: send
moa[6]: run
moabu[2]: dark
moatah[7]: pigeon
mockra[5]: rain
modda: stone
modla[2] (mooller): nose
moerlina: friendly spirit
moerpun[2]: take care of, watch
moerty[3]: canoe
mogo[5]: axe; stone
moilong: advancing tide
moilwer[3]: stars
moinpunden[2]: kiss
moiya[6]: bullroarer
mokari[2]: new
moki[2]: cloudy
molbangen[2]: warm (verb)
molbangimindin[2]: warm oneself
moldar[2]: breath
moliagulk: wooded hill
mollineux[3]: man

molta (molltee[8]): wrist
moltu[4]: night
moma: ghost
momar[4]: father
monatandra[2] (munathandra): teeth
mongan: a mammal
mongana (ammonga): fly, insect
monkeit[4]: make
monmondik[4]: girl
monomeeth: agreement, benevolence, enjoyment
monoro[6]: eye
monti[6]: stork
mooaloonyah[7]: pigeon
moochambilla: kangaroo
moocoo[8]: heel
moodai[5]: possum
moodla: corroboree
moodunna: finish (verb)
moogaray[5]: hailstone
moogana: white-breasted shag
moogra-ba (moograbah): bell-magpie, black-backed magpie, crow-shrike, or donkey-bird
moola: shady place
moolgewanke: bunyip
mooller[4]: see modla
moolyera[8]: curlew
moomowroong[4]: pebble
moona[2]: plenty
moondah: beyond
moondak: squeeze (verb)
moondara: periwinkle
moondani: embrace (verb)
moonga[8]: dark
moongan[4]: father
moonoon: see mooroon
moonoroo[6]: eye
moonthalie: ourselves
Moora: spider which brings girl babies to earth

mooro-moora: good spirit
moorang[4]: cloud
moorapoo: back
mooregoo[5]: mopoke
moorelli: thirsty
moorillah: see morilla
mooroo: bitch
mooroocoochin[4]: black swan
mooroola[5] (mooroolah): waddy (weapon)
mooroolbark: red bark
mooroomin[5] (murroomin): bark of kurrajong tree
mooroon[5] (moonoon, moornin): emu spear; fat
mooroop: spirit
mooroopna: deep hole
mootcha: native cotton bush
mootta: wood
mooyi[5] (mouyi): white cockatoo with yellow crest; also the pointers of the Southern Cross
mopa[5]: no
morala: see morgalal
morallie[2]: low (of cattle)
morang[4]: sky
moranjee[8]: steady
morannie[8]: relative
morequirta[8]: see morquita
morgalal[3] (morala): sea
morilla[5] (moorillah, morillah): stony ridge
mornee[3]: rain
morokkun[2]: bring, get, hold, obtain; sieve
moroko[5]: sky
moron[5] (morrun): live (verb)
morquita (murequirta): hat
moru[2]: below, down, go down, go
moruga[2]: sweet
moruldun[2]: adultery

morwong[5]: carp, jackass fish
motepa[5]: child, girl
motthari[2]: steal
motu[3]: one
mouyi: see mooyi
mowan[3]: sun
mowantyi[2]: pine tree
moye[3]: sun
mrangalli[2]: stony ground, place full of stones
mree[4]: eye
mubbo (mubboo): beefwood tree
mubboon: small tributary
mubbu[5] (mubbo, mubboo): beefwood tree
mudla[2] (mutla): nose
mudlo[3]: head
mugana: willy wagtail ('teller of tales')
muggil[5]: stone knife
mukka[2]: no
mulali[2]: bone
muldarpe: devil-devil, evil spirit
muldi[2]: bough, foliage, leaves; smoke
muldurie[2]: magpie
mulga: acacia
mulgamurra[8]: blowfly
mulgar naggaman[1] : cold
mulla-munale[6]: throwing stick
mulla-murrale[6]: boomerang
mullara[5]: cloud
mullauna: together
mullaya[5] (mullayerh): companion, friend, mate
mullee mullee[5]: dream spirit (or wirinun)
mullian[5] (mullyan): wedge-tailed eagle
mullian-ga[5] (mullyangah): morning star
mullo[6]: stone

mulloka[5]: water devil
mulloona: each other
mullyan: see mullian
mullyangah: see mullian-ga
multara: covering of emu feathers used for warmth in cold weather
multuwallin[2]: many
multuwarrin[2]: too much
mulundar: swallow (bird)
mulwala: possum grass
mulya: nose
mumalwar[3]: blood
mumberleya[2]: live (verb)
mummjeeli[8]: take, take it
mummu[2]: good
mumnunah[6]: mouth
munainpulun[2]: languid
munangpallan[2]: soft
munathandra[2]: see monatandra
munda[8]: earth
mundamunda: string ornament
mundara[4]: thunder
mundarra[8]: garment, shirt
mundawora: native blackberry
munde-wudda[5] (mundehwuddah): north-west wind
mundho[4]: mouth
mundi[2] (munde): man's breast
mundil[6]: night
mundill[6]: big
mundoe: big toe
mundooie[5]: foot, leg
Mundook: goddess or spirit of fertility
mundroola: two only
mundurra: hunter
munengk[2]: lip
mungaiyin[2] (mungaiyulun): write
mungaiyuwun[2]: tattoo
munganye[2]: again
mungara[2]: thirst, thirsty

mungedma[3]: wife
mungeenie[8]: pick up
munggai[2] (mungow): close (to the person spoken to), near
munggaiyuwun[2]: cut the body
munggan[2]: in that
munggar: tattoo marks
munggi[5] (mungghee): mussel
munggi-wurray-mul[5] (mungghe-wurraywurraymul): seagull
munggow[2]: in there, there
mungi[2]: eat; message stick
mungi[3]: child
mungkule[2]: lake
mungoon-gali[5] (mungoongarlee, mungoongarlie): goanna
mungow[2]: see munggai
mungrie[2]: see munkuripa
mungunni: evil
munguwun[2]: feed (verb)
muninyeri[2]: moustache
munja[4]: fish
munjong: new chum
munker[2]: small hawk
munkora: dilly bag
munkumbole: clever, expert, superior person
munkuripa[8] (mungrie): three
munmunde[2]: barter
munnari[2]: short-tailed goanna
munniger[4]: he, it, she
munnura[6]: mouth
munta[8]: sand
munte[2]: thumb
munthu[2]: kangaroo
muntye[2]: lame
munung[4]: hand
munyarai[2]: see minyai
munyertoo[2]: cold
munyeru: small, black edible seeds
muralappi[2]: little, young

murang[6]: fish
muranpun[2]: seize
murde-ejit[3]: hill
murdu: totem
mure[2]: dust
muremelin[2]: quick
murga muggai[5] (murgah muggui): trapdoor spider
muri[3]: sun
muritpun[2] (muriltpun): close shut, shut in (verbs)
murna[2] (murnna): big, great, many, much
murndiella: wave
murra[2, 5, 6, 8] (marra, murrah, murramamlunya): finger, hand
murrai[5]: good
murrakeen[5]: girl
murramai: talisman made of quartz crystal
murramaner[4]: we
murranudda (merrenetta): bustard
murrara[2]: duck
murra-wunda[5] (murra-wondah, murrawundah): climbing rat
murree[5]: fish
murri[5] (murry): many, very
murri[6]: kangaroo
murri: hand, root, or cavity which holds water
murri-cooler: fiercely
murr-nong[2]: plant with edible root; yam
murromin: see mooroomin
murrumbidga: big water
murrumbinner[4]: you
murrumbooee: waterfall
murrumbung: pleasant
murrumnuller[4]: they
murrun[4]: see moron
murrunmil[2]: hurry

murry: see murri
murta[5]: husband
murtama[5]: your husband
murtee[8]: knee
murti[5]: my husband
muruke[6]: day
murule[2]: mosquito
murungar[2]: steady
murunkun[2]: cool
mutla[2]: see mudla
muttun[2]: drink (verb)
mutto[6]: boy
muttun[2]: smoke tobacco
muttura[5]: land
muwe[2]: sleep
muwe watyeri[2]: sleepy
muwityiwallin[2]: wakeful
mya[1]: hut
myall: wild, wild man, untamed, stranger. In a modern sense it has come to mean amateur or new chum
myee: native, native-born
myhee[8]: bread
myimbarr: black wattle
mying myrongatha[4]: eye
myndee: sycamore
myndie: see mindi
myneam[4]: moon
myorli: small red kangaroo
myrna (minnear): food
myrniong: cooking place

N

nacooma: see!
nagga[1]: cold
naggi[3]: dog
nagooroo[2]: see
nai-ari: mountain devil
nainkulun[2]: depart

naityi[2]: alone
naiya[6]: hold on to
naiyuwe[2]: that there
naiyuwun[2]: curse, scold, swear
najan[4]: mother
najina[2]: see
naka[6]: water
nakame[5]: name
nakelang[4]: see
naki[6]: eyes
nakilli[6]: see
nakkare[2]: black duck
nakkin[4]: see
nak our[2]: look out
nalgarmyeri[2]: bull ant
nalgo[1]: teeth
nalin[2] (nalurmi): lightning
nallak: come on
naltra[5]: how many
nalurmi[2]: see nalin
nam[2]: us, we two
nama[6]: teatree
namaga[6]: pearl shell
namagan[4]: see
namana[5]: see namarra
namarra[4] (namana): mother
nambucca: winding river
nameropinah[5]: hole in the side
namma: breast. A nammahole is a well or water hole
nammana[2]: sit
nammin[2] (merammin): cook (verb)
nammuldi[2]: hidden, unknown
nampulun[2] (nanampundun, nampundelin): conceal, hide
namtuk[4]: husband
nanampundun[2]: deny, persuade
nanampundun: see nampulun
nananook: behind
nanarinyeri[2]: sandlfy
nanarlin[2]: flat

nanauwun[2]: look round
nanbean[8]: eyelash
nanbimba[8]: eyebrow
nanbundelin[2]: caught
nanbundun[2] (nanbundun): catch (verb)
nandalie[5] (nandale): fire
nandroya: man and wife
nangalla[5]: fall, sit
nangana: see
nangare[2]: shelter
nangarikelerad[3]: three
nangkero[5]: pelican
nangoran[4]: husband
nangurwallin[2]: exult
nanni[2]: I
nannygai: snapper
nanowande[2]: hooked stick for pulling banksia flowers
nanowie: corner
nantoo[8]: thirsty
nantuma[5]: bend (verb)
nanwai[5]: canoe
nanyee[8]: womb
nanyima[4]: play (verb)
napa[5]: I
napa[6] (nopa): water
napalle[2] (nape): husband
napanopa[6]: water
napowatyeri[2]: married man
nappa[5]: I
napwallin[2]: marry
nara[5]: companion. (yato nara: his companion)
narahdarn[5]: bat
narana[2]: hear
narang: little
narbeethong: cheerful, lively
narcoolba[8]: ashes
narcoonah[4]: see
nardu (nardoo): clover fern, a plant with edible seeds

nare[2]: tame
naretha[4]: salt bush
nargarawarat[3] (nargilwarat): three
nargarik[3]: two
nargariknargarik[3]: four
nargoneit[4]: hear
nargoon: native bear
nari: my companion
naripal[4]: spear
narkindie[8]: cave
narkale[2]: thumb
narkowalle[2]: his mother
narluk[2]: see ngalluk
narluke[2]: half full
narmar[8]: grass
narmare[2]: spring of water
naroa-mine[6]: man
narr[2] (ngarr): distinct, intelligible
narrah[4]: sea
narrawa: spring water
narrinyee[8]: breathe
narrinyeri[2]: people
nartee[8]: spring of water
narteol[2]: small piece
natan[6]: fig tree
natoah[5]: me
natto[6]: I
naweenda: fine day
na-wo[5] (gnahwo): yes
nauwe[2] (nauwurle): whose
ndruila[6]: native companion
neanga[4]: sit
neanwert[4]: sit
neanya: fly (insect)
neecoo[8]: elbow
neeghinee[3]: sit
neelong: bone
neena[7]: you
neenjeweny[8]: kiss (verb)
neenca[8]: sparrow
neerim[4]: hut

neetee[8]: fat
neeyangarra: eagle
neilyeri: pointing bone or stick
nemmin[2]: leave, leave off, stop
nemmuran[2]: remain
nenartin[2]: spread
nenengkin[2]: fall backwards
nenggatauwe[2]: pliable
nent oura[2]: out of the way
Nepelle: ruler of the heavens
neppaldar[2]: three
nerambo: against
nerbungeron: grand-father
nerndaik[4]: teeth
nerndoa: teeth
nerntoma[5]: more
nerntulya[5]: well, hole in the
    ground
nerreman: river bend
netangee[3]: yours
newchin[8]: sneeze
ngadhungi[2]: bewitch, charm
    (verb)
Ngaetelli: evil spirit which
    inhabits the black cockatoo
ngai[1, 6] (ngaia): I
ngaiambin[2]: return
ngai-i[2]: I
ngaikung[5]: eye
ngaitshi[2]: mine
ngaityapalle[2]: grand-mother
ngaitye[2]: friend
ngaiyeri[2]: father
ngaiyuwun[2]: abuse (verb)
ngak[2]: almost
ngake[2]: close (adj)
ngalata ngillel[1]: we
ngalluk[2] (narluk, narluke): half,
    half-full
ngama: bottle-shaped pits in rock
    for holding water
ngammaura[5]: mother

ngan[2]: me
ngan[5]: who
nganauwe[2] (anauwe): my
nganden[2]: cause to fly, frighten,
    scare
ngangan[1]: mother
ngangaranden[2]: cry out
ngangga[1]: sun
ngangge: see ngongi
ngangor[1]: star
nganmil[1]: me
nganna[6]: they
nganni[1] (ngan indi): who
ngarakkani[2]: shark
ngaralin: linger, wait
ngarari[2]: log
ngarbinya[2]: lie down
ngarlengarl[2]: small branch
ngarma[5]: they
ngarneit[5]: see
ngarningi[2]: fig
ngarntin[2] (ngartin): fly (verb)
ngarpin[2]: sorry
ngarr[2]: see narr
ngarra[2]: daughter (form of
    address by mother to
    daughter)
ngarraraipari[2]: ship
ngarrin[2]: build, make
ngarring[6]: boy
ngartang[6]: mother
ngarte[2]: river bend, corner
ngartin[2]: see ngarntin
ngathungi: instrument used in
    witchcraft
ngauandi[2]: nest
ngauka[6]: see
ngauwire[2]: son
ngauwun[2]: pass (verb)
ngeane[5] (ngeen): we
ngele[2]: heart
ngembelin[2]: spin

ngempin[2]: twist
ngende[2]: darkness
ngenempin[2]: grind
ngenna[5]: he, it, she
ngenyarin[2]: stare
ngeragge[2]: scrub
ngerake[2]: teal
ngerakowun[2]: overturn, turn inside out
ngeri[2]: fishing net
ngerin[2] (ngirin): catch fish with a net
ngerla[2]: fine
ngernka[2]: beard
ngerwein[4]: sun
ngiakkai[2]: armpit
ngiampi[2]: backbone
ngia ngiampe: bond between families or tribes
ngibalin[2]: paddle a canoe
ngikunde[2]: tadpole
ngilde[2]: cobweb
nginbundim[2]: flee
ngindai[5, 6]: you
ngingeranggi: cough
nginno[1]: sit
ngipi[2]: shell
ngio[4]: I
ngiralin[2]: open (intrans verb)
ngirin[2]: see ngerin
nglaiye[2]: grass tree
nglalin[2]: as, like, resemble
nglelin[2]: grope with the feet, know
nglelurumi[2]: faith
nglulun[2]: top
ngodli[2]: we
ngoinkun[2]: shiver, tremble
ngoiyir[2]: promise (verb)
ngoiyun[2]: farewell
ngokkun[2]: disappear
ngolika: wattle flower

ngolkun[2]: bite (verb)
ngolun[2] (ngolamindin): wear (verb)
ngomerna[2]: go
ngommi[2]: convicted, guilty
ngomon[1]: big
ngongi[2] (ngangge): what, who
ngontha[2]: bad
ngoppano[2]: uncle on mother's side
ngoppun: move, step (verb)
ngopuld[2]: walk (verb)
ngorkulle[2] (ngokulli): bright, flame
ngottha[2]: me
ngowalle[2]: go
ngowalour[2]: go!
ngoweyin[2]: destroy
ngrakkuwallin[2]: angry, growl (verb), passion
ngraldi[2]: rage
ngrallin[2]: cure
ngramal[2]: open!
ngrammin[2]: open (intrans verb)
ngranyeri[2]: wonderful
ngraye[2] (ngragge, ngraldi): anger
ngrekkaldo[2]: tomorrow
ngrelggi[2]: contrary
ngrelggimaiyi[2]: contrary wind
ngrengkulun[2]: cough (verb)
ngrilkulun[2]: dance (verb)
ng'rui moch: native cat
ngruinyerar[2]: much more
ngudela[5]: see nguobela
ngunkurawallin[2]: go before
ngruwar[2]: abundance, abundant, all, many, much, whole
ngthummulun[2]: green
nguba[1]: blood
ngubbo-numma[5]: this
nguldamul-mindin: tire
nguldammulun[2]: tired

ngulde[2]: animal food, flesh, muscle

nguldin[2]: finish (verb)

nguldun[2]: cure, healthy

nguldunguldelin[2]: fist fight

ngulli[2]: long ago

ngullun[2]: remember

ngultun[2]: bruise, hit with fist, kick

ngumba[5]: mother

ngumperi[2]: milk, nipple

ngumpura[2]: woman's breast

ngumundi[2]: black snake

ngune[2]: vegetable food; you

ngungango[4]: he, it, she

nguni[2]: tea

ngunggurank[2]: before (in front of)

ngungyen[2]: kindle, light

nguobela[5] (ngudela): sit

ngupe[2]: down (of bird)

ngura[2]: hut, house, or shelter of any kind

ngurangpar[2]: brain

ngureng[5]: ear

ngurintand[2]: many times

ngurle[2]: mountain

ngurle[2] (ngurleuwar): you two

ngurnauwe: our

nguroo[2]: hair

nguruguldun[2]: knock

ngurukwar[2]: outside

ngurukuwarrin[2]: last (final)

nguta[6]: black

ngutam[6]: banana bird

nguwa[5]: give

nguyanowi[2]: cousin

nhamba[6]: we

nia: here, this

nidja[1]: this

nielongan[6]: mother-in-law

nierrina[7]: hawk

nihooloo[8]: me

nilee: bush rat

niley[5]: shell

nillam[4]: bad

nimi[2]: mouth

nimmitabel: souce of many streams

ninder[5]: heavens

nindethana: ours

nindoah[5]: you

nina[2]: see ningana

ningana[5] (nina): fall, sit

ninkaiengk[2]: pair

ninnai[6] (ninna): sit

ninnann[8]: sit down

ninndwer[5]: we

ninwoa[5]: he, it, she

niu[2]: I

njugur: see wunjugur

noa[2]: husband

noinpalin[2]: soft

noiyulun[2]: I grope with the feet

nokarugge[2] (nolkaruggi): locust

noko[6]: water

nokuna[2]: look

noma uwe[2]: yours

nompie[6]: wedge-tailed eagle

nompulun[2]: plant (verb)

nonedia[5]: cousin

nonga[6]: kurrajong tree

nongo[5] (nonjo): woman

noojee: content

mooko[6]: give

noonameena: sleeping place in the bush

noondha: at

noonga[5] (noongah): kurrajong tree; him

noora-gogo[5] (noorahgogo): orange and blue beetle

nooroo: quick

nooroobunda: morning

nooroonooroobin: see nuru-nuru-bin

noorumba: hunting ground

noorwanang[4]**:** nose

nootoo[8]**:** chin

nopa: see napa

norabeetya[7]**:** green

norachanda[4]**:** make

normananyee[8]**:** snore

noro[5]**:** three

note[4]**:** cloud

nowaiy[2] (nowaiy ellin): none, not, nothing

nowantareena[7]**:** sister

nowego[4]**:** sun

nowieya: there

noyang: eel

nruwi[2]**:** a cold

nuba[6]**:** you

nucka[5]**:** eat

nucko[5] (nukou): water

nukee[5]**:** one

nukung[5]**:** woman

nulgerong: moonlight

Nulgine: bird goddess

nullanulla[5] (nullahnullah): club with heavy head

nullar[8]**:** forehead

nullegai: we two

nullgoonie[8]**:** bite, eat

nulu-gail[5] (gnooloo-gail): white painted headband

Nulu-yoon-du[5] (Gnoolooy-oundoo): monster of legend

numald[2]**:** secretly

num-ba-di[5] (numbardee): mother, maternal aunt

numbe[2]**:** chin

nummunin[4]**:** heat

nunbalo[5]**:** to be drowned

nunden[2] (nunten): suspect

nunga[6] (nungge): day

nungana: cause

nunggaiyi[5]**:** wife

nungge[2]**:** see nunga

nunggi[2]**:** fishing line, rope

nungheenah[7]**:** elf, fairy

nunghungee[8]**:** look out

nungkutu[1]**:** give

Nuninjeeri: old man of the black frost

nunkalowe[2]**:** light (noun), sunlight

nunkardeol[2]**:** short club or waddy

nunkeri[2]**:** beautiful, excellent, good, handsome, pretty, right, tasty

nunkeri-mari[2]**:** right hand

nunkowallin[2]**:** being good

nunkuluthen[2]**:** running water

nunkumbil[6]**:** morning star

nunnoo[5] (nyunnoo): grass shelter

nunta[4]**:** bad

nunten: see nunden

nunthy[4]**:** he, she, it

nunungki[2] (nunukke): flour, fruit

nunyin[5]**:** see

nura[5]**:** you

nurawordubununa: carpet snake

nurong: bread

nurriga[6]**:** moon

nurroobooan and **nuroolooan:** see nuru-buan

nurrumbeek[4]**:** I

Nurrumbunguttia: old spirits who were responsible for darkness, storms, and evil spirits

nurrumpi[4]**:** native bear

nurrungar: listen

nuru-buan[5] (nurroobooan, nurroolooan): south

nurula pundi[5] : club

Nurunderi: teacher sent by the Great Spirit
nuru-nuru-bin[5] (nooroon-ooroobin): south wind
nuta[6]: night
nutam[6]: banana bird
nuttoo: grub
nyamopulun[2] (nyampundun): walk softly
nyang[4]: sit
nyangow[1]: see
nyauwe[4]: sun
nyenkulun[2]: dissatisfied
nyenkundun[2] (nyiukundun): cross (ill-tempered), offended
nyerin[2]: cry (verb); depend on; expect
nyerpulun[2]: pant
nyiddin[1]: cold
nyinna[6]: sit
nym[3]: child
nyrangkin[2]: burn (verb)
nyringgen[2]: singe
nyrippin[2]: clean (verb), wash
nyumap bottyu[1]: small
nyungie: moon
nyungu[6]: Torres strait pigeon
nyurang[1]: you

O

oba[3] (obait, obaitj): water
obernilimer: whistle (verb)
odenpa[8]: ironbark tree
odern[1]: sea
odneler: midnight
odunepa[8]: white ant
ohi[3]: woman
oiyangopan[6]: carpet snake
ojalli[3]: fire; tree
ojena[3]: fire; tree

okolyer[8]: cloud
olba[8]: red ochre
old-burra[8]: dust
ol-dorry-e-way: kiss
oleara[8]: string
olebrya[8]: south
olemunda[8]: dust
ollo: brown bee
olltoo[8]: nostril
olono[3]: hill
oloorinann[8]: shame
oltarkim: broke
olumbera: swear
omalwin[3]: kangaroo
omenderry[8]: chest
omil-dadgee[8]: bamboo, large reed
onak[3]: earth
onbellera[8]: whirlwind
onengarkwa[8]: starve
onya[6]: ghost
Oobi Ooobi[5]: sacred mountain in Bullima where Baiame lives
ooboon[5]: blue-tongued lizard
oodoolay[5]: rain-making stone
ooeena[7]: fuel
oogee: head-dress
oola[5] (oolah): red prickly lizard
Oola-pikka: imaginary tribe which lives at the back of the south wind
ooliekirra: bright, clean, new
oolyarra: young man
oomborra[8]: maggot
oomoomurla: superior
oompi: see humpy
oompi bong: deserted camp
oongarra: asleep
ooraa[8]: see oura
ooranye[2]: rainbow
oorgker[3]: heat
oorla[2]: camp, hut, nest

ooroowinannee: grey owl; also daughter of Merpulla the rain woman

ooya[5] (ouyah, ouyarh): quarrian parrot

ooyan[5] (ouyen): curlew

ooyella: compassionate

ooyu-bu-lui[5] (ouyouboolooey): black snake

opera-yenpa[8]: bark (noun)

orad[3]: earth

orialk[3]: two

orialkeraroka[3]: three

orana[3] (korana, orani): moon

oridji[3]: sea

orinjetta[8]: spark

orodina: chin

orojiimul[3]: nose

orowa medinda[3]: sea

orra curra: desert oak; large owl

orrapoora[8]: magpie

orucknurra: large fire

orumbera: large spear

otama[6]: porpoise

otayba[8]: bird

oticha: half

otorkweta[8]: heart

ottinna[8]: hot

oura[8] (ooraa): wood

ouraka: wait awhile

ourapilla[8]: black

ouratita: black beetle

ouyah and **ouyarh:** see ooya

ouyen: see ooyan

owadema[8]: more

owingee: he, hers, his, it, its, she

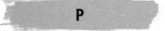

P

pademelon: scrub wallaby

padewer[8]: go

padewappa: I go

padewaimba: you go

padewaley: we go

yato padewa: he goes

padilpa[8]: parrot

padmur[2]: point (noun)

padmuri[2]: sharp

padmurwallin[2]: pointed

padmurwarrin[2]: sharpen

paiala[2]: cold

paialla[5]: tell

paieri perna[2]: big

paipan[6]: black ibis

paipe[2] (paiapowallin, paiapulun): stiff

paitcha: breast, anything that develops with maturity

paiyin[2]: hate

pakapaka[6]: bullroarer

palberry: corruption of word for native currant

paldharar[2]: hail

paldi[2] (palli): by and by, future

pallai[2]: while

pallarang[4]: bow down

palli[2]: see paldi

palpera[8] (palperipa): leaf

palthawangalana[5]: ashamed, naked

   palthawangalnappa: I was ashamed

   palthawangalnimba: you are ashamed

pama[6]: man

pan[6]: liquid

panamuna: ocean

panda[5]: heart

pandana[5]: spear (verb)

pandappure[2]: gun

pandelanen[5]: tired

   pandelnappa: I am tired

   pandelnimba: you are tired

pandin[2] (panden, plunden): carry in the arms, embrace, lift, nurse on the knee, seize, embrace

panelgorana: be noisy, speak
panelgorappa: I speak
panelgorimba: you speak

pangalarke[2]: eldest daughter

pangali[2] (panggalli): eldest son

pangari[2]: shade, shadow, soul

pangarinda[2]: evening, twilight

panggalli: see pangali

panichie[4]: wife

panimillie: small river

panitya[4] : area of land

panje: black-eared cuckoo

panketye: boomerang

panpande[2]: cherry tree

pantin[2]: two people sleeping together; squeeze

papa[6]: teat

pappa: seed food

pappora[5]: appear

parattah[7]: frost

Parawanga: spirit of madness which appears in the form of a mirage

parehana: all

pargi[2]: wallaby

pariwilpa[2]: heavens

parlcoon[8]: tattoo

parn[4]: water

parnggi[2]: deep water

parnta[2]: see burnta

parpin[2]: cry (verb), sorry

parpinga[6]: father

parpin mewe[2]: anxious, desire (verb), yearn

parpun[4]: mother

parra[2]: hair

parragilga: narrow-leaved ironbark tree

parru (barrow): fish

parrumbal: mushroom

partambelin[2]: wrestle

partin[2]: rub

partumbe[2]: infant

partyi (partch): shoal

parumin[4]: rain

pateenah[7]: egg

patter[2]: eat

patya[6]: flower

patyuwarrin[2]: cure

pecan[4]: hand

pedgery: see pitchery

peer[8]: mouth

peggeralin[2]: dream (verb)

peggerambe[2]: breakfast

pehah[5]: bone

pek: empty; very

pekeri[2]: dream

pekin[2]: empty (verb); finish

pelberri[2]: tea

pelberrimunt[2]: lungs

pelde[2]: musk duck

pele[2]: greedy

pelepe[2]: land

pellati[2]: edible grub found in banksia

pempin[2]: give

pendin[2]: smell

pengana[7]: hawk

penghanah[7]: ford

pentin[2]: decayed, stinking, withered

peppee[3] (pipee): father

pera[5]: club

peranbim[2]: divide amongst, share

perar[2]: fingernail

Perindi: mythical yellow-brown striped goanna

perke[2] (perki): hole, large hole; steep

perlka[5]: fishing line
pernmin[2]: flick
pertill-lerra[8]: cheeks
pertorrue[8]: string
peta[2]: tree
petachall-lily[8]: scorpio
petamalde[2]: thief
petcheual[4]: two
petcheualenea[4]: three
petcheual-petcheual[4]: four
peti[2]: frost
petin[2]: refuse (verb)
pettin[2]: abduct, steal
petye[2]: face
pewingi[2]: swamp hawk
piallano[4]: die
picca[8]: sore
pichi-malla[8]: come on
pidne[6]: hear
piealah[4]: girl
pierah: : see pirra
piggi-billa[5] (piggie-billah): ant-
    eater; echidna
pikuwa[6]: salt-water crocodile
pilar[5]: spear
pilbe[2]: dirty
pilbiwallin[2]: dirty
pildin[2]: drive
pilepi[2]: dew
pilgeruwallin[2]: see pulkeri
pilkundun[2]: frown; stare at
pillambe[2]: black cockatoo
pillara: spear with two barbs
pilli: see billa
Pilliethillcha: aurora australis
pillcoo[8]: vein
pill-ler: spit
pilpati[2]: hip
piltengi[2]: hard, strong
pilyaulun[2]: man
pilyan-undun[2]: shake the head
pimble: country, district

pimpa[5] : tree
pimpala[5]: pinetree
pinah[5]: hole
pinaroo (pinarroo): old man
pinbittulun[2]: push (verb)
pindan[1]: desert
pindattulun[2]: lay an egg
pindyin[2]: pick out
pinera[5]: climb
    pinerappa: I climb
    pinerimbo: you climb
pinggen: throw down
pinggi[2]: seaweed
pingkin[2] (pinggen): cause to fall,
    fall, overthrow
pingyin[2] (pindyin): find
piningi[2]: buttock
pinjaroo[2]: make
pink-hi: holiday
pinna[8]: ear
pino[6]: female ghost
pinpan[8]: lightning
pinpi[6]: parrot
pinpin[2]: push; put
pinpuna: share (verb)
pinta: bamboo spear
pintamin[2]: carry off, take away
pintannie[8]: open
pintapinta[8]: moth
pinterry[8]: star
pinyali: emu
pintyin[2]: pick up
pinyatowe[2]: sugar
pinyin[2]: see pingyin
pinytowe[2]: honey
pipa[6]: father
pipa: bent
pipee[3]: see peppee
pipi[2]: egg
pipipa[6]: sandpiper
piralko: native companion
pirilah[4]: cold

pipirbin[6]: small
pirra[2, 6] (pierah): moon
pirramurra: shield
pirri: small leaf-shaped spear point of chipped stone
pirria[2]: clay
pirriwee: possum skin rug
pirron-yallock: little water
piruwallin[2]: breathless, dead, fainted, insensible
pita[6]: bamboo spear with four points
pitchery[5, 6] (bedgery, pedgery, pitchiri, pituri): shrub, the leaves being used as a narcotic
pitchie: wooden vessel used for holding water
pitchingga: gum of pine or gum tree
pitereka[5]: white
pitja[4]: fire
pitoa[5] (pito): moon
pitti[2]: line
pityi[2]: cape, headland
pitura[5]: light
piyaller: speak
plaityinggin[2]: proud, vain
plangge[2]: drum made of skins tightly rolled and beaten by the hand
pleppin[2]: feel
plewalauwun[2]: grope in the dark
plomare[2]: ice
plombatye[2]: deaf
plombatye[2] (plomb atye wallin): disobedient
plombewallin[2]: stupid
plongge: club, knobbed weapon for inflicting punishment
plorte[2]: egg yolk
plotye[2]: childless woman

plowallin[2]: cramp; lament (verb)
plunden[2]: see pandin
plurampe[2]: valley
poenghana[7]: ringlets
pogal[3]: head
poi: dust
poka mala[5]: lie
pokkoremin[2]: heap up
pola[6]: paternal grand-father
polgumpi[2]: backbone
poli[3]: man
pollit[4]: two
pollit kepap[4]: three
pollit pollit[4]: four
poltha[2]: see pultha
pombulun[2]: flow; leaf
pomeri: mudfish
pombindho[5]: earth
pompo: egg
pomponderoo[5]: land
ponda[4]: stone
ponde: Murray cod
pongo: flying squirrel
pooet: treefern
pookanah[7]: albatross
pookerah[4]: heat
poolkrinna: mischievous spirit
poolooloomee: firework made of gumtree bark
poomong: tin
pooney[8]: blow (verb)
poonganyee[8] (poonganie): hit, kill, strike
poonja[8]: sing
poonta buckanee[8]: heavy
poontee[8]: grub
poora: tail
poork[4]: head
poorlie[2]: stars
poorp[4]: kill
poorparta[2]: sparrow-hawk
poortge[6]: heat

pootikkatikka: wattle-tree
poottoo[4]: land
popa[4]: blow, shoot (verb)
popogina[5]: gun
pordenpar: calf of leg
porle[2]: child
porlta[2]: possum
porn il[2]: died
pornumindin[2]: kill
pornun[2] (pornunil): dying; like (verb); love
pornurumi[2]: death, death-causing
poroany[8]: press (verb)
potoroo: kangaroo rat
potyanambe[2]: food for a journey
pouraller: mist
powdingella[6]: cold
powenyenna[7]: magpie
poymalangta[7]: kill
poyyou[8] (puya): smoke
prakkin[2] (prakour): rise (verb)
prandyi[6]: butter-fish
pranggiwattyeri[2]: tiger snake
prangpin[2]: diarrhoea
prantin[2]: start (jump with fright); wonder
premin[2]: tie (verb)
prempun[2]: cook (verb)
preppin[2]: lift, raise
pretella[6]: moon
prewarrar[2]: rib
prewirri[2]: side
prilde[2]: ant
prildin[2]: pursue
prilpulun[2]: spring of water
pringgarimmin[2]: tie (verb)
pritye[2] (prityin): firm
prityururmi[2]: strength
proi: big
prolggi[2]: brolga; Magellan Clouds
prolin[2]: red

prumpun[2]: drive flies away with smoke; prepare an oven
pruwuttar[2]: pieces
Puckowe: the grandmother spirit
pudding-ball: corruption of name for a fish
puka: see bucka
puka[6]: baby
pukara[2]: heat
pulca[8]: toe
puldan: see pultin
pulhiner[6]: dying
pulkeri[2] (pilgeruwallin): greedy
pullatye[2]: two
pulley[8]: stone
pulliner[6]: die
pullun[2]: bathe, swim
pullybuntor[8]: mountain range
pulpilla[4]: heavens
pultera[5]: canoe
pultha[5] (poltha): bark, covering, skin, skin garment
pultin[2] (puldun): receive, take
pultue[2]: weak
pultuwarrin[2]: rot (verb)
pulwaiya[6]: totemic ancestor
pulyara: long-nosed rat
pulyugge: ball, ball game
pumdo[5]: smoke
punauwe: kangaroo skin bag
punde[2]: bag
Pundel: another name for Baiame
punden[2]: childbirth
pundeol[2]: mouse
pundi: dog
pundira[6]: conch shell
punga[6]: hut
punjil: finger
punka[8]: large lizard
punkerri[2]: brown duck
punkulde[2]: fish spear
punkunduleol[2]: bandicoot

punkunduli[2]: bandicoot rat
punnamoonta[7]: emu
puntaman: fishing net
punthari[2]: scrub
puntin[2]: arrive
puntyaiya[6]: swamp turtle
puppa[8]: dog
pupperimbul: diamond firetail or spotted-sided finch
puratte[2]: black and white shag
pure[2]: waddy
purinyeriol[2]: wild man
purkabidni[2]: ghost, spirit
purni[2]: oven
purni ngomerna[2]: come here
purnung: dingo
purpuck[4]: cold
purpuk[4]: head
purragia[5]: lie (falsehood)
    purragiappa: I tell a lie
    purragimba: you tell a lie
purreung[5]: day
purri[2]: hill; kidney
purrinunggi[2]: right hand
purroin[4]: night
purtia[2]: kangaroo rat
purtin[2]: hurt
puthawing[2]: lower arm
putta[8]: grass; lazy
puttheri[2] (putte): end
puttun: pinch (verb)
puya[2]: see poyyou
puyulle[2]: emu wren
pyabea[4]: woman
pyala[4]: tree
pyingerra[6]: pine tree

Q

quabara: sacred song
qualpar: large rat

quandong: native peach tree
quarail[4]: big
quarallia[8]: star
quarragwan[4]: heat
quasha[8]: water
quasha-booga[8]: small water
quasha-iperta-quorna[8]: deep water hole
quasha-unjewma[8]: drink
quasha-ul-kurry: rainy sky
quasha-undema[8]: rain (verb)
quasha-yerra-pichica[8]: swim (verb)
queeabraabra[3]: who
queeal[3]: foot
queenguarr[3]: nose
quear[8]: crooked, no good useless
queearr[3]: hand
queeneeda[3]: fire
quei: little girl
quei-marla: big girl
quei-marla[8]: adolescent girl
quei-marla-goobita: adolescent girl
quemilla[3]: tongue
quillagee[3]: big
quinja: ash
quorna[8]: deep
quunder[3]: club

R

ragaralti[2]: egret
raiaralin[2]: flow, overflow
raiaramin[2]: pour
rammin[2]: inform, tell
rampaullun[2]: persuade someone to go with the speaker
randi[2]: widower
randli[2]: childless father, father who has lost a child

ranwul[2] (rande): ancient, old
raraityungun[2]: beg
rarkee: bush food
rata: plant, vegetable
rattulengk[2]: mother and child
rawadabir: see awadabir
rawan[3]: rain
rawlinna: wind
rekaldi[2]: water rat
relbulun[2]: suffer
rengbari[2]: stop
retulengk[2]: father and child
retyinne[2]: heel
rewuri[2]: spring (season)
reyin[2]: show
reytyunggun[2]: ask
reytyuwundun[2]: forbid to accompany
riawena[7]: games
riawunna[7]: circle
rikkara[2]: south
ringbalin[2]: chant, sing, song
ringmail[2]: hunger
rogoona[7]: forehead
roka[3]: one
ronggi[2]: brother-in-law
rongummun[2]: bark (verb)
ronumdo[5]: boy
roragarin[2]: shake
rorari[2]: rotten
rumalduwallin[2]: joke (verb)
rumaiy[2]: west
runde[2]: cousin, friend
rupulle[2]: chief, land-holder
ruwe[2]: land

S

saleng[4]: tongue
shoo-ho: death word
su[2]: curse, expletive, or imprecation

T

ta[6]: land
taa[6]: foot
tackan[4]: see
tagera: cockle
taikundun[2]: cry out
tainbarilin[2]: arrive
tainke[2]: swamp
tainki[2]: salt
tainpulun[2]: forget
taipan[6]: brown snake, rainbow snake
taitpullun[2]: jump (verb)
taiyi[6]: maternal grand-father
taiyin[2] (tarraiyin): command, go away!, send
takkin[2]: eat
takkure[2]: plucked
taldauwin[2]: squeeze out disease or sickness
taldree[5]: young man
taldumande[2]: house, substantial house
taldumbarrin[2]: hold (verb)
talga: sow-thistle
talkinyeri[2]: bustard turkey
talkiwallin[2]: cross (ill-tempered), miserable
tallaim[6] (talla): tongue
tallangge[2]: tongue
tallara[2]: rain
tallarook: wattle bird
tallawong: bell or black magpie, donkey bird, or crowshrike
tallbee[8]: wet
tallerk: thistle
tallon[4]: see tully
tally[8]: sandhill
talpa[2]: ear
tamba: ibis

tambelin[2]: choose
tambur[6]: mouth
tampin[2]: walk
tana[6]: stand up
tandan: catfish
tang[2]: where
tangari[2]: edible gum
tangulun[2]: stand
tanpundun[2]: put together
tantan[6]: cold
tantin[2]: lie down
tapang[4]: father
tapangk[2]: near, near you
tappak: bronze-wing pigeon
tappan[6]: stake
tappenitin[2]: yawn
tappin[2]: fierce
tar[8]: mouth
taralye: throwing stick
tarangk[2]: between
taranna[7]: wallaby
taree: tomahawk; wild fig
tareena[7]: basket
tari[2]: opening
tarkee: evil spirit in the form of
    a woman who drinks blood
tarki: perch (fish)
tarkoori[2]: bittern
tarlarang[4]: red-billed plover
tarlina[5]: see therlinya
tarlina[6] (tarlina aitye): one
tarlina barko[6]: three
tarlit[4]: small
tarlo bra womba lettie[4]: boy
tarloorin[8]: yawn
tarl worcat[4]: girl
tarmaroo[6]: possum
tarnalo[2]: never
tarno[2]: not
tarntunnerrin[8]: tired
tarra[4]: white
tarraiyin: see taiyin

tarralangi[6]: see therlinya
tarrangower: rough; high hill
tarrgoorn: reed necklace
tarrinyeri[2]: middle one
tarrukengk[2] (kurrengk): leg
tartar burlke: hair
tarte[2]: younger brother
tartengk[2]: stick for beating time
    in singing
tarti[2]: younger sister
tata[6]: frog
tatea[6]: whistling duck
tatya[6]: goanna
tauel[2]: neighbour, neighbouring
    tribe
tauo[2]: don't, no!, not
tauwa[6]: talk
tauwangi[2]: firestick
tauwin[2]: lean on
tchaceroo[6]: magpie
tchaik: an expression of
    contempt; unreliable person
tealedyan[6]: shark
tean[6]: take
teangi: earth
teepookana[7]: kingfisher
teeta: ant, insect
Teetya: swallow which brings
    boy babies to earth
teeya[2]: teeth
teeyar-tarlina[6] (teeyir-tarlina):
    see therlinya
tekin[2]: escape
tellingiter[3]: one
tempi: swamp duck
tenan[4]: foot
tendi[2] (thandi): decision of the
    elders in council
tendu[2]: climbing frog
tenjumar: drink (verb)
tepi[2]: live (verb)
tergoonee[2]: sit

teriltin[2]: pluck feathers
terninyeri[2]: boot
terpulun[2]: appear, come in sight, come out of, emerge
terrara: place of shrubs
tete: kingfisher
tewart: see tooart
thacka[5]: bank
thackory[5]: heavy
thadelee[2]: sea
thalaak: sow-thistle
thalan[4]: tongue
thalera: manhood, strength
thalinya[2]: therlinya
thalme[2]: bay
thambaroo: spirit; also in some parts the name for a white man because he is believed to be the reincarnation of a spirit or someone who is dead
thame[2]: shallow
thammi[2]: seashore
thandi[2]: see tendi
thandwalla: gumtree on the edge of a river
thanga[2]: down
thankomalara[5]: island
thanpathanpa: snipe
thappin[2]: open (to make a hole in)
tharalkoo: duck
tharamba[4]: make
tharook: convolvulus
theen-who-ween: an ancient, legendary name for the platypus
therlinya (tarlina, teeyar-tarlina, teeyir-tarlina, thalinya): tongue
therna-perty[5]: kidney
therto[5]: head
thetthere[2]: dray (a word which comes from its movement)

thiar[4]: land
thickathickana[5]: pour water into a vessel
thidna[2]: see thina
thidnamura: toad
thiewie: flowers
thilhya[5]: strong
thina[6]: ear
thina[5] (thidna, tshina): foot, footprint, track
thinana: beside
thindu[4]: this
thingairipari: spear belonging to a medicine man
thirti[2]: mean, selfish
thirlta[6]: kangaroo
thirtawalla[2]: head
thita thata lana: itch
thockyar[6]: land
thoma talko[4]: good
thonku mundil[5]: night
thooma: sandhill creatures which belong to the Dream Circle
thoomie: peace, silence
thoopara: native pear tree
thoorka[4]: big
thopramolla[5]: get inside, get on, sit on
thorom[5]: smoke going up a hollow tree
thowla: spoonbill duck
threttin[2] (threllin, trattin): divide, part, split
thriggi[2]: message stick
thrintin[2] (thrinden): pluck
thrippin[2]: sprinkle
throkkun[2]: throw away, toss
throttun[2]: attack one man, place, put down
thrumari[2]: cape (point of land)
thrunkkun[2]: go away!
thrunkun[2]: frighten

thuckara[5]: river bend
thuiye[2]: stump
thulanja[5]: bad
thuldi[2]: pus
thuldun[2]: meet
thulga[5]: bad
thulloo-munal[6]: camp
thulloo-nurral[6]: hut
thulti[2]: floating mass of reeds
thultie[2]: ear
thumelin[2]: green
thummyerloo[6]: sun
thumpun[2]: hunt (verb)
thunbira[2]: mouth
thundarta[5]: nothing
thungana[5]: fill up a hole
thungge[2]: see tunge
thungy[4]: land
thuppun[2]: carry
thur[2]: truth
thurakami: swim
thurkuna: swimming
thurar[2] (thure): straight
thurre[6]: sit down
thurto[5]: head
Tickalara: spirit world, hereafter, happy hunting grounds
tiddalick: frog
tidnah[6]: foot
tiendi[1]: star
tier[4]: live (verb)
tiewiwar: see tyiwewar
tikki[6]: live (verb)
tilpulun (tilpuldun): cracking of lice, crackling of flames, sparkling
tiltili[2]: pied crow shrike
timbelin[2]: smoke tobacco
timpin[2] (timbelin): lick (verb), tasty
tinabulka: boot
tinar[5]: woman

tingin[2] (tinkin): stoop
tingowun[2]: inform, tell
tinka[2]: day
tinkelin[2] (tinkin): swell (verb)
tinna-punni: bone carried in dilly bag to repel evil
tintauwa[6]: black snake
tin-tookie: gnomes who inhabit the bush and hear the last words of those who are dying
tin-tuppa: imaginary plant people
tinuwarre: bream
tipi[6]: guts; root
tipuldun[2] (tipundun): break in pieces, crush
tikeri[2]: knot
tirkundun[2]: dive
tirra[4]: teeth
Tirtelak: sacred frog who guards underground rivers
titna[2]: foot
tittadi[2]: flea, vermin
tittimballin[2] (tittimbarrin): tickle
tityarokan[6]: willy wagtail
titygan[4]: die
tityowe[2]: death-adder
tiwiwarrin[2]: fast, speedy
tjukaro[2]: kangaroo
tjurunga (often corrupted to churinga): sacred object of wood, stone, or shell
tloppere[2]: ibis
tlopulun[2]: grope in the mud for crayfish
tluiye[2]: short
tluyeol[2]: shortest
tokai[5]: night
tokiejonburnba[8]: bulldog ant
tokkun[2]: crowd, pinch (verb)
tokorauwe[2]: narrow
tolai[2]: beardless

tolkun[2]: poke, stamp
tolkundun[2]: stab
tolloiyer[3]: two
tomin[2]: swallow hastily
tonaleah[7]: sun
tonde[2]: blind
toney[8]: thunder
tonga jija[1]: ear
tong kongka[5]: early morning; evening
tooart (tewart): tuart gumtree
toogaadya[2]: small
toolangatta: many kurrajong trees
toolain: brown wattle
toolka: Cape Barren goose
toora[4]: woman
toorange: jealous
toorlie: poison stick
toorutbambam[4]: die
toota[4]: star
topyrun[2]: star
torarin[2] (torauwun): assemble, collect
tore[2] (torengk): mouth
tortuwallin[2]: delay, quiet, silent
totolar[5]: hill
tottumbarrin[2]: eat meat and vegetables
tottung[2]: disappeared, out of sight
Totyargeril: the star Aquila
tour-ur-rong: good grass
towa: bladder
towarnie[8]: dig
towera[4]: fire
towulun[2]: blaze (verb)
towun[2]: tread
trandararin[2]: divide amongst
trangkin[2]: drive away
trata[6]: night-fish
trattin[2]: see threllin

trawalla: much rain, wild water
trelin[2] (tremin): tear, torn
trelin ngreye[2]: dawn
trippin[2]: drip, drop (verb)
tshina[2]: see thina
tshinta[2]: sun
tshuppana[2]: kiss
tuan: flying squirrel
tuat[4]: fish
tuckatuck[8]: tickle
tuckie: see tukkie
tuckonie: little man of the forest
tudhuki[2]: bed
tuki[2]: bullfrog
tukkeri: flat, silvery fish forbidden to woman
tukkie[2] (tuckie): bream
tuldar[2]: star
tuldi: forequarter
tuldin[2]: net (verb), surround
tulgeen[2]: put together
tullangapperi[2]: mat
tullun[2]: howl (wind); scrape
tully[5] (tallon, tullon): tongue
tulpi: 'talk stick', used for tapping out messages
tultun[2]: chip (verb)
tuma[6]: fire
tumakowaller[2]: swan
tumaquoi[2]: look
tumbe[2] (tumbelin, tumbewallin): alive, live (verb)
tumbe an ngulde[2]: raw meat
tumbeelluwa: evergreen
tumbetin[2]: heal, save
tumbi[2]: raw
Tumbutilamaldi: Saviour
tummun[2]: choke, hiccough
tumpinyeri[2] (tump): life (belong to life)
tumpun[2]: count
tundi[2]: spark

tunge[2] (thunggi): ankle
tunggar[2]: joint
tunggerar[2]: language
tunggare[2]: word
tungge[2]: wrist
tuni[2]: ground
tunka[6]: day, month
tunkeri[2]: louse
tunkun[2]: fondle, nurse
tunkuwallin[2]: play (verb)
tunta[6]: spear
tunte[2]: middle
tunthun[2]: rejoice
tupong: marble fish or freshwater flathead
tupun[2]: guard
tura[5]: spear
turelin[2]: cover up
turika[8]: bone
turi kalkir[2]: covered
turlemindin[2]: frightening
turlin[2]: frightened
turnar[2]: toe; track
turni[2]: hand
turninyeri[2]: shoe
turnit[1]: boy
turokkul[2]: lame
turrammelin[2] (turramulun): make a noise
turro[2]: fire
turrumturrum[6]: rain
turt[4]: star
turtangi[2]: knee
turuwun[2]: guard
tuta[6]: parrot; palm leaf
tuu[6]: spear with three prongs for spearing bony bream
tuyalie[6] (tuyalie-dusali): teeth
tuyulawarrin[2]: look for, seek
Tya: Earth; flowering time
tyalli[4]: tongue
tyarbuk[4]: mouth

tyarmorak[4]: you
tyelde[2]: clay
tyele[2] (tyerle): upper arm, wing
tyeli[6]: swamp fish
tyelokuri[2]: mussel
tyelyerar[2]: ray of light, sunbeam
tyepi[2]: quail
tyerle: see tyele
tyetyin[2]: annoint
tyilye: fly, maggot, worm
tyilyi[2]: rice
tyinkulun[2]: screech
tyintin[2]: remain in one place
tyinyeri[2]: child
tyirpin[2]: deny
tyit[6]: fish hawk
tyiwallin[2]: become dry
tyiwar[2]: loud
tyiwewar[2] (tiewiwar): hurry
tyiwi[2]: dry
tyiwiwallin[2]: withered
tynrmeargorak[4]: we
tyrilly[4]: heavens
tyrintyin[2]: sneeze
tyurmik[4]: I

U

ua[4]: give
uaburika (umburika): centipede
ubeeterra[8]: fog
uc-aliebra (ucaleebra): reed
uckillya[8]: brother
uc-neer[8]: father
uc-nulla-mull: swing
ucnullya[8]: dog
uc-nun-alemem: shake
ugundyi[6]: crab
uka[6]: white sand snake
ularit[3]: star
ulbra-cullima[8]: claw

ule²: wave (noun)
ulla: well
ulluricna⁸: dirty water
ulpirra: flute; love-horn made of hollow sticks
ulwai⁶: paternal grand-father
umanbang⁵: make
umbacoora⁸: baby, child
umbee-leedin-gorra⁸: kneel
umbeeramalla⁸: tired
umbellditta⁸: orange tree
umboa: urine
Umborn-ditchalicka⁸: a fabulous female being who lives in mountain ranges and cures people of their ills. It is also the name for a red stone which is powdered and put on wounds to heal them
umburika⁸: see uaburika
ummal³: foot
ummee³: sun
umorra⁸: rat
umpara⁶: stingray
umpiya⁶: water-lily
unchurunqua: painted finch
uncoo⁸: sleep
unda⁶: see ungda
undarnga: bush food
undeanya⁸: see undeneya
undee-lablab⁸: butterfly
undeneya (undeanya): wasp
undia: gap, gorge
undie⁵: teeth
unditter (unditta): stink
undooeata (hundoeta): string
undoolya³: shadow
undunga: wet
undurra³: silver wattle
unengoo²: they
ung²: after
unga²: see ungooroo

ungai²: to, with
ungamala³: sea
Unganti Barachi⁴: 'the land beyond the sky'
ungarunya: rush
ungawilla: black magpie
ungda (unda): he, she, it
ungee-gungee (ungee-gunjee): grasshopper
unggoingee³: I, we, us
ungiverta: crooked
ungjeeburra⁸: crane
ungolar: native currant
ungooroo² (unga): give
ungroo²: hear
ungun²: if
ungunai² (ungul, ungunel): before (of time)
ungunuk²: when
ungunyer-pollipa: shoulder
ungurgal³: sea
ungwarlyer: medicine
ungwyndei⁸: sleep
ungwyner⁸: yours
unja: mating fever
unkee²: woman
unkeegeega²: girl
unmaturra⁸: hungry
unmerta⁸: buckbush
unnee²: who
unoyie: broad-leaved tea tree
unti⁸: run
untita: down feathers
untoo⁸: windpipe
unya⁸: louse
upmoa⁸: snake
upmurra⁸: camp
uralla: big hill; by-and-bye; camp; running water
uran⁶: heat
urdera⁶: sand ridge
ure⁶: ear

urnin[3]: woman
Uroo: mythical water snake
urpalk[3]: sky
urra-quarra: grey goose
urrie urrie[5]: soul
urtathurta: shoe
urumi[2]: see arami
urungari: bees' nest, sugar bag
utam[6]: corpse
utyana[2]: initiated youth
uuna[4]: sun
uwa[6]: leech
uwan[6]: meet
uwinnia (geewinnia): mosquito
uwoppa (youwoppa): spider
uworra[8]: road
uwurta[8]: bush wallaby

W

wa[6]: give
wa-ah[5]: shell
waaljerrumbuddy kewat[4]: spear
wacka[5]: chin
Waddahgudjaelwon: see Walla-
 gudjail-wan
waddy: war club, also used for
 any stick for striking. There is
 a theory that it is the
 aborigines' pronunciation of
 the English word 'wood';
 another that it is the
 Tasmanian word 'wi' (wood,
 or fire), with a modifying
 particle
wadelang[2]: tree
wadleena[2]: bad
wadna[2]: boomerang
wah: an exclamation
wahgoo[5] (whagoo): game of hide-
 and-seek

wahgunyah: place where crows
 are found
wahl[5] (euahl, youal): no
wahler[5] (wahlerh): manna which
 runs down the trunks of trees
wahn[5]: crow (the most
 mischievous of all birds)
wahrang[1] (warhrang): three
wahroonga: see warooga
wahroonga: our home
wai-i[2]: afraid, fear
waiirri: heavens sky
waikerdumai[6]: hill
waimba: you
wainbaru[2]: rain
wainkan[6]: curlew
waiye[2]: light brown snake
waiyin[2]: drive
wakaje: emu
wakbok[3]: head
wakerdi: crow
wakka elji[2]: small
wakkalde: shield
wakkin[2]: spear (verb), wound
 (verb)
wakkin-turtangk[2]: kneel
wakoola: girdle of human hair or
 kangaroo skin worn by men
 who have been initiated
wakulun[2]: caw (verb)
wal[2]: place (noun)
wal[3]: ear, hear
wala[6]: blue-tongued lizard
walbeeatta[8]: see wolbitta
walkandi[2]: north
walla: jump (verb)
walla-boondie[5] (wallahboondee):
 topknot
wallaby (wallabee, wallobi,
 wolloby): small kangaroo
Walla-gudjail-wan[5]
 (Waddahgudjaewon,

Wallahgudjailwon): female spirit, guardian of unborn spirit children

wallahboondee: see wallaboondie

Wallahgudjailwan: see Walla-gudjail-wan

Walla-guroon-bu-an[5]: the messenger of Baiame, guardian of male spirit children awaiting birth

wallangar: burnt stump

wallaroo[5, 6]: large species of kangaroo

walla-walla: jump quickly

wallin[2]: accompany, hang, pendant

walloobahl: see wallu-barl

wallong: pounding stone

wallowa: broom wattle

wallu-barl[5] (walloobahl): barking lizard

wallung[4]: stone

walmat[3]: rain

walpa[5]: lift

waltra[4]: fire

waltye[2]: childless father, father who has lost a child

wamba[1, 3, 6]: white man who lives with aboriginal woman

waminda: companion, friend

wanappe[2]: mushroom

wanbanalong: place where kangaroos are found

wanbanna: lack of understanding, stupid

wanbin[2]: pity (verb)

wanda: sandhill

wandelana[5]: chin

wandoo[1]: wandoo gum

wane[4]: moon

wanga[5]: see manba

wangarang: tortoise

wangin[4]: boomerang

wangkin[2]: ascend

wangoora[6]: baby

wanji: bird dance

wanka[6]: dilly bag

wankin[2]: ask, beg

wankin mewe[2]: pant

wanna: digging stick

wanni[1]: die

wanowe[2]: paternal uncle

wanta[6]: discard

wantan[6]: leave tracks

wantyandyindan[6]: spear with three prongs for spearing bony bream

wantya pian[6]: young married woman

wanya[4]: boomerang

wanye[2] (wunye): then

wanye[2]: mountain duck

wappilka[5]: hot

war: up

wara[6]: oyster

warama: dugong

waranyukbeal: large gum tree

wararuwnaji[3]: child

warat[3]: one

waratah: tree with red flowers

warbang[4]: canoe

warde yallock: big water

warea[5]: small

warhrang[1]: see wahrang

wari[3]: head

wariat[3]: stone

wariatanbirik[3]: hill

wari-comomo[3]: woman

wariga[4]: hear

waring[4]: sea

wariya: string of wombat or wallaby hair

warka[6]: tortoise

warkolala[4]: two
warkolala boor[4]: three
warkolata-warkolata[4]: four
warma: stop a while
warna[2]: sea
warooga[5] (wahroogah): child
warra[1]: bad
warra[2]: over there
warraba: see wayamba
warrah: honeysuckle
warrain: belonging to the sea
warralewar[2]: see warre
warramba: see wayamba
warrambool[5]: flood water on
    polygonum flats; Milky Way
warrame[2]: left hand
warrannie[8]: sing
warrang[6]: bad
warra-nunna[5] (warranunnah,
    wurranunnah, wurrunnunnah):
    bee
warraroong: hillside
warratinnah[7]: sky
warrawee: come here
warre[2] (warralewar): high, high
    up
warreeah: mountain ash
warreen[4]: sea
warreen: wombat
warregal[4]: dog
warrew[8]: wallaby
warreyin[2]: follow
warridanga: midday
warrie[6]: dog
warrigal: dog, i.e. dingo; later
    used as a word meaning wild,
    and then applied to wild
    horses, wild men, etc.
warri-kundall[6]: dog
warrina[6]: give
warring: the Galaxy
warringa[4]: sea

warritsha[2]: emu
warriuka[2]: boat, ship (from warr
    ngukatha, lit. wind go)
warriwillah: twisting water
warroo[4]: kangaroo
warroo[6]: boomerang, day
warroo[8]: fire
warroo-culla[8]: moth
warroong[4]: dew
warr-ringa[8] (warringobeeny):
    cold
warruc-color: see color
warta[2]: wallaby
Warte[2]: Venus (planet)
wartin[2]: track (verb)
waru[2]: see woora
warwanbool[4]: growing tree
wata[6]: crow
watangrow[2]: yesterday
watnah[6]: boomerang
wato[5]: take hold
wattangger[2] (wattangerind):
    evening
wattar[2] (wattangri): twilight
wattora[8]: long
watye[2]: polygonum shrub
watye[4]: man
watyin[2]: have
waukatte[2]: small hawk
wauwakkeri[2]: grey hawk
wauk-wauk-wa: pigeon
waukyn warra[1]: bad
wauwauwi[2]: fear
wayamba[5] (warraba, warramba,
    wayambah, wayambeh,
    wayembeh): turtle, tortoise
waybung: chough (bird)
waycoot: much
wayembeh: see wayamba
waylehmina[7]: swallow (bird)
waywa[5] (waywah): belt worn by
    man, made of possum sinews

with pendant strips of
paddymelon skins
wayway[5]: devil's bread fungus
weagolalameit[4]: die
weagoon murmbool[5]: live (verb)
wee-ar[8]: none
weedah[5]: bower bird
weehi: boy
weekin[4]: die
weelar[8]: stomach
weeloo[8]: curlew
weelya[7]: parakeet
weema[8]: small
weenduga[8]: goanna
weeombeen: see wi-oombeen
weerap: blackfish
weeriga: fire-walking
weeronga (werona): quiet, rest,
sleep
weeroona: resting place
weeyehr[3]: nose
weeyer[3]: tongue
wee-y-tena[7]: rainbow
weing[4]: fire
weire[4]: mother
wela[6]: barter shell
welappe[2]: mullet
weloorarra[8]: west
welya[4]: summer
wenbener[3]: throwing stick
wenjoitj[3]: kangaroo
wenkana[2]: speak
wenkin[2]: refuse (verb)
wenyerang[4]: child
wepe: quiet
werderh: west wind
werendun[2]: lead, pull
werentun[2]: answer (verb)
werguttulun[2]: fish (verb)
weringerong: lyre bird
werite[4]: banksia
werkin[2]: fish (verb)

wernma[8] (wonma): long way
werona[4]: see weronga
werrilah[4]: cloud
werring[4]: car
werrook: root
werrup: red ochre
wertun[2]: skin (verb)
wertuwallin[2] (wurtuwallin): sweat
(verb)
werunnunn[4]: dog
wettinnie[8]: hold (verb)
weumpa[8]: no
weya[3]: hair
whagoo: see wahgoo
wherto[5]: old man
whilpra: aborigine's
pronunciation of wheelbarrow,
applied also to carts and
wagons
whinya[4]: where?
whippoo[8]: tail
whitkitha[6]: girl
whytalla[8]: tell
wi[5]: clever; fire; a small fish;
wood
wia[2]: mother
wi-bulloo[5]: fire; women who
lived in a country where there
was no fire
widawok[3]: big
widdidna: truffle
wiena[7]: firewood
wietatenana[7]: nautilus
wiinki[6]: arrowroot
wiitii[2]: sting (verb)
wika[6]: speech
wikky: bread
wilari[3]: star
wildin[2]: stare at
wilga: dogwood, willow, (always
known as wilga)
wilgee: yellow clay

wilgu-wilgu[5] (wilgoo-wilgoo, willgoo-willgoo): painted stick with feathers at the end

wili[2]: pelican

willa[2]: wife, woman

willang[4]: rain

willanjo[5]: boy

willarra[6]: tomahawk

willawallin[2]: stubborn

willawatta-thuyin[6]: woman

willkilla[4]: look round

willum[4]: hut

willy-willy: storm, whirlwind

wilpa[2]: cloud

wilpy[5]: camp (verb)

wiltcha[2]: night

wiltja: hut, shelter

wiltun[2]: spread

wilyango[5]: boy

wima[2]: four

wimmera: uncle

wimmin[2]: work

wimouyan: clever-stick

winamin[2]: beat time

winani: hollow tree

winberongen[8]: whistle

windarra: where?

windawityeri[2]: bullock

windtha: grey owl

wingamin[2]: sow

wingaro[5]: see

winin[2]: deceive, lie

wininaru[2]: deceit

wining: live (verb)

winkulun[2]: whistle

winkundun[2]: breathe, blow a fire

winmin[2]: make

winni[2]: be off

winnea[4]: they

winninger[3]: day

winnungi[5]: hear

winta[2]: spear

winthunga: somewhere

winyangun[6]: man

winyar[6] (winwar): big

winyer[4]: who

wi-oombeen[5] (weeombeen): small bird like a robin redbreast

wipa[6]: wash up against

wirake[2] (wiraki): friend, mate

wirakulun[2]: bleat

wirildar[2]: an acacia

wirin[2]: ache, hurt (verb), ill

wirinun[5] (wirreeneen, wirreenun, wirrinun): 'clever man', medicine man, sorcerer

wirlpa[2]: hare

wirngill: koala

wirpa[2]: ant

wirrah[1]: fish

wirralee: gin fish

wirrangi[2]: wrong

wirrannie[8]: scratch (verb)

wirrap[4]: fish

wirratye[2]: childless mother, mother who has lost a child

wirree[5]: vessel for holding water, made of bark and shaped like a canoe

wirreebeeun[5]: adolescent girl, young woman

wirreecoo: tea-tree

wirreeneen: see wirinun

wirrelyerna: level ground

wirre-oobra: 'dust shadow' which indicates that no water is present

wirrie: stick inserted in dead body

wirrinun: see wirinun

wirritin[2]: rough

wirrullummi[2]: itch (noun)

wirruna: sunset

wirtoo[6]: big

wirwy[4]: I
witchetty: edible grub
withinka[2]: green frog
wititurar[2]: small snake
witjuti: acacia
wittha: leg
witwit: throwing stick
wityeri[2]: fig leaf
wityungyin[2]: overcome, press
   heavily
wiwieringgere[2] (wiwirringille):
   native pheasant
wiwirremalde[2]: doctor
wiwirimalde[2]: sorcerer
wiwirri[2]: pain, sickness
wobbegong[5]: carpet shark;
   snapper
wobma[2]: snake
woga[4]: give
woggara[5] (woggarah): wooden
   axe used in fighting
wogghee and **woggigai:** see
   woggi
woggheeguy: legends (stories
   from the plains)
woggi[5] (wogghee, woggigai):
   plains
woggoon[5]: mallee fowl
woggul: sacred water snake
wohn[6]: night
woka[6]: swim
wolbah[4]: hill
wolbitta (walbeeatta): billy
woldra[2]: heat
wolka[6]: spear with stingray barb
wolka[8]: drawing, painting; ice
wolkolan[6]: bony bream
wollomai: snapper
wollombi: meeting of the waters
wollowra[8]: eagle
wollumbin: high mountain
wolpa[8]: wind

wolter (wolta): rib
woltsha[2]: eagle
womah[6]: boomerang
womba[5] (wombah): deaf; mad;
   the star Canopus
womba[8]: knife
wombalano: beautiful; love
wombat (womback): a marsupial
wombul[5]: sea
womma: fat, colour of fat
wommee[8]: snake
wommera: see woomera
wommurrur[5]: throwing stick
wompa[2]: hill
wompinie: sheltered from the
   sun
wondah: see wunda
wonenie[8]: fall (verb)
wonga[5]: bulrush; pigeon
wongalyer[3]: what, which, who
wonga-wonga: pigeon
wongguri[2]: ring-tailed possum
wongoonoo[8]: grass
wonka[8]: spider
wonkana: sing
wonma: see wernma
wonna[8]: stick
wonnewarra[8]: hold on
wonninny[8]: throw
wono[3]: sky
wonthaggi: pull
woodgera: daylight
woolladge-ilkna[8]: milk
woollung[5]: hard
woolta[2]: heart
woomelang[4]: poor
woomera (wommera): throwing
   stick
woonah[6]: lie down
woonda[1]: shield
woongarra: sleeping place
woora[6] (waru): kangaroo

woorail[4]: lyre bird
woorak[6]: honeysuckle
woorak: plain
woorarra: mountainous place
woorawa[6]: wedge-tailed eagle
wooremolleen[4]: day
woorin[4]: sun
woorinyan[4] : affection, love
(verb)
woorkarrim: blue
woornack: sunshine
woorookool: fine weather
wooroonga: sea
woorree: sea
woorun[4]: day
woorwoorr[4]: sky
woowookarung: plentiful
worippa[6]: storm bird
workat[4]: woman
worlba[2]: boy
wornkara[2]: crow
worooa: green
worpa[6]: nest
worraworra: fighting stick
worru[4]: mouth
worrue[8]: wood
wotiya[6]: yam
wrack[4]: land
wring[4]: ear
wruwallin[2]: hope (verb)
wu[6]: fire
wuka[6]: flying fox
wulde[2]: wedge-tailed eagle
wulgaru: devil-devil, made from
a wooden figure
wullaki[2]: black cockatoo
wullanti[2]: string bag
wullun[2]: blue sky
wullundigong: goblin, little man
of the bush
wunba: fin
wunbi[2]: puppy

wunda[5] (wondah, wundah): ghost,
evil spirit, white person, white
devil
wunde: long heavy black spear
wundurra: warrior, young man
wune[5]: give
wungghee: owl
wunggi: seashore
wunjugur[6] (njugur): well
wunmullun[2] (wunmun): stretch
out the hands
wunmun[2]: throw
wunta[8]: fish
wun-u-wa-tirring[4]: sunrise
wunye: see wanye
wur[6]: fire
wuralparin[2]: stir
wurang[6]: bad
wurchiewurchie: white owl
wurdawurda (wurtawurta): band
made of emu feathers
wurgulin[6]: short-legged kangaroo
wuri[2]: red gum tree
wurley[5] (wurlie): hut, shelter
wurranunnah: see warranunna
wurrawilberoo[5]: whirlwind,
whirlwind devil; Magellan
clouds
wurrook: flat
wurrunnunnah: see warranunna
wurruntun[2]: crush
wurruwallin[2] (wurruwarrin):
believe
wurtawurta: see wurdwurda
wurte[2] (wurtuwallin): wet
wurtun[2]: warm (verb); feel
(verb)
wurtuwallin: see wertuwallin
wurtherama: hurry (verb)
wutta[6]: dog
wyah[5]: an exclamation
wyang[2]: second

wyebo[4]: small
wyebokooron[4]: canoe
wyeera: dig (verb)
wyehoota[8]: possum
wyelangta[7]: large timber
wyena[7]: small timber
wyeriguru: spirit of fire
wyerow[1]: make
wyirre[2]: white of egg
wyralla: black and red cockatoo
wyterrica[8]: wattle
wyuna: clear water

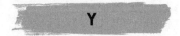

ya[2]: yes
ya[3]: teeth
yabber: talk
yabbie: small crayfish
yabm-irriti: quarrel (verb)
yackan[4]: mother
yackatoon: happy
yacker: see yakka
yackhoo[8]: mother
yacki: celebration, big noise
yago[1]: woman
yaitcha: yes
yakake: bathe
yakalya[5]: break
yake[5]: cold
yakea[5]: widow
yakka (yacker): work
yakkai[2]: ah! oh!
yakkoeela[6]: father
yakoolabarri: place where water lilies grow
yalabidji[3]: hand
yalakki[2]: carpet snake
yaldeenie[8]: come back
yalgin[2]: soak
Yalkara: spirit of drought

yalkin[2]: full; wet
yalkuldun[2]: melt
yallaban[4]: native raspberry
yallambee: live at, stay
yallane[2]: mat
yallara: long-eared bandicoot
yallart[2]: flock of emus
yalta[8]: charcoal
yam[2] (yammin): other
yaman: speak
yamba: see humpy
yambalin[2]: play at cat's cradle
Yammacoona: female ruler of sky spirits who made rivers on earth
yammalaitye[2]: one
yammamel[2]: one more
yamma murru[6]: hand
yammiam[2]: each
yammin[2]: see yam
yamminuwar[2]: another one
yammin uwar korn[2]: foreigner
yamminye[2]: another
yan[5]: go
yandala[6]: spear with a long point
Yananamaka[6]: 'Trample the hair', the first man child to be created
yandarlana[5]: cry
yande[2]: old, useless
yanedana[5]: unfasten
yanga[6] (yanganna, yangena): mother
yangalla[6]: sit down
yanganna and **yangena**: see yanga
yangatin[6]: native cat
yangennanock[4]: all of us, we
yangoora[4]: stringybark tree
yangor[1]: kangaroo
yanima: will you?
yanka[6]: tail

yankulun[2]: loose
yanmulun[2]: drip, drop (verb)
yannathan: walk (verb)
yanning[8]: walk (verb)
yant[2]: peace
yan yean[4]: unmarried man
yap[3]: fish
yapar[2]: stick
yape[2]: tree
yapinga[3]: big
yappera[5]: camp
yappulun[2]: enter
yappundun[2]: bring in
yara[6]: seagull
yaraan[5]: white gumtree
Yaraandoo[5]: Southern Cross
  (place of the white gumtree)
yarakai[5]: bad
yaral[2]: when?
yaramin[2]: pour, spill;
yarran[5, 6] (yarra): bear, hair
yari[2]: what?
yarild[2]: how
yarluke[2]: path, track
yarn[4]: water
yarnde[2]: spear
yarngge[2]: vein
yarnimindin[2]: talk
yarnin[2]: saying, speak
yarnirumi[2]: conference,
  discussion
Yarra: spirit woman of the sand
  storm
yarra[4]: hair
yarra: speak (verb); tree
yarra: see yaran and yarrah
yarraga[5]: see yarrageh
yarrageh[5]: south-east wind;
  gentle spirit of spring
yarragerh mayrah: spring wind
yarrah: river red gum (but also
  applied to many trees)

yarrak: fight (verb)
yarraman: horse (from yeera—
  teeth; mahn—long)
yarramba[4]: throwing stick
yarran: an acacia
yarrara[5]: wood
yarraringy[5]: possum
yarrawah: storm of wind, gale
yarrawonga: nesting place of
  cormorants
yarra yarra: ever-flowing
yarri: native bear
yarrum[5]: throwing stick
yarrumba[5]: boomerang
yartamin[2] (yartin): stretch out
  the hand to receive anything
yartin[2]: stretch a skin out to dry
yarto[5]: wind
yartuwe[2]: big girl, young woman
yarumpah: honey ant
yarunmundule[2]: bat
yataotbidji[3]: teeth
yato[5]: he, his
yatta[4]: good
yattoo[4]: live (verb)
yatye[4]: bad
yauoanggi[2]: porpoise
yawoma[5]: come back
yayin[2]: chew, eat
yea[6]: mussel
yeatoura[5]: who
yeera[5] (yiera): teeth
yeildo[2]: blood
yelga[2]: dog
yelka[4]: dog
yelka: mouth; yam
yellawa[4]: day
yelpia[5]: count (verb)
yelpulun[2]: deceive, lie
yenamalde[2]: enemy
yenara[5]: that way
yenben guala[4]: man

yenembelin²: wrestle
yenempin²: entangle, twist
yenpar⁸ (yenpa): skin
yentoo⁸: you
yeppa²: hole
yepperta: deep
yera⁴: teeth
yeramba: sugar ant
yeranda⁵: black cockatoo
yerang: thicket
yerdlee²: man
yergutta⁸: bag
yerhillgar⁸: liver
yerilla: ground
yerlata²: oyster
yerlieyeega²: boy
yernd⁵: stone
yerra: ant
yerracharta⁸: spear
yerracolya⁸: water vessel, also
    used for carrying babies;
    made from a hollowed out
    piece of bean tree
yerra-coppa: desert oak
yerrakincha: disease
yerrawar⁸: boomerang
yerrear⁸: salt bush
yerricknar⁸: blood
yerta²: land
yertauwullar²: remain
yetni²: he, she, it
yetto²: good
yeyauwe²: hungry
yeyeko³: small
yeyen³: hand; teeth
ygo¹: I
Yhi⁵: sun goddess
yhuko⁵: sun
yhuko hippy⁵: sunset
yhuko pappora⁵: sunrise
yiallinah⁴: sit
yiarculrer⁴: teeth

yiarrih⁴: mouth
yiera²: see yeera
yikkowun²: enough
yikowalle²: his father
yilgi²: salt water
yilin²: broken
yiltoo⁴: blood
yinai⁵: boy
yinbaikulun²: go away
yindi: sun
yingge²: wool
yingoorna: today
yirtuggi²: bucket
yirum⁶: woman
yityumbarrin²: carry on the
    shoulder
yluppun²: to bring fire
yoldi²: black shag
yolla⁷: mutton bird
yondun²: wade
yonga¹: give
yongga⁴ (yonggadyr): sun
yonguldye²: darkness
yooralanni: will love
yooralla: love
yoorami: love (verb)
yoorana: loving
yoothapina: good luck
yorlin²: go into deep water
yorlun²: descend, come down
yorte²: winter
youa⁴: throwing stick
youal: see wahl
youamalla⁸: throw
youayah: see yuaia
youhi⁸ (youi): give
youko: see yuroka
younger⁴: give
youngoloy⁵: swan
youracudda⁴: hear
youria⁴: ear
yourula (youroul): bullock's horn

youwoppa[8]: see uwoppa
yowi[5] (yowee): soul, spirit,
   warning spirit of death
yowi[5]: yes
yoyangamalde[2]: champion
yoyangi[2]: bed; fight (verb)
yrottulun[2] (yuruttulun): thin
yuaia[5] (youayah): frog
yuka[2]: stand
yuka[6]: tree
yuke[2]: boat
yukkay[5] (yuckay): an exclamation
yukunder[3]: kangaroo
yul-arai: satisfied
yulde[2] (yullukke): tall
yulthi[2]: bark of tree
yultun[2]: draw towards, drag,
   lead; save life
yultuwarrin[2]: mix
yulu-mara[5] (euloomarah): grub
yulu-wirree[5] (euloowirree):
   rainbow
yumbera[2]: fly
yummun[2]: stand
yun[2]: by and by
yunbeai[5]: familiar spirit,
   individual totem

yunde[2]: down (feathers)
yune[4]: man
yungana[2]: cockatoo
yungara[2]: wife
yunka[6]: make
yunkara: stranger
yunkimp[4]: canoe
yunkundun[2]: extract
yunt[2]: crowd, together
yuntheyunthe[5]: kidney fat
yuntuwarrin[2] (yuntuwallin):
   assemble, crowd (verb);
   useless
yuppun[2]: arrange, lie down,
   place
yuppundelin[2]: dress (verb)
yuri[2]: ear, hear
yurlunggur: rainbow snake
yurnga: extensive view
yuroka[6] (youko): sun
yurru[6]: cloud
yurruttulun: see yrottulun
yurung[6]: rain
yutthero[5]: road
yuwam[6]: black snake